LEARNINGEXPRESS

THE BASICS MADE EASY . . .
IN 20 MINUTES A DAY!

A New Approach to "Mastering The Basics." An innovative 20-step self-study program helps you learn at your own pace and make visible progress in just 20 minutes a day.

GRAMMAR ESSENTIALS, 2 ed.
HOW TO STUDY, 2 ed.
IMPROVE YOUR WRITING FOR WORK, 2 ed.
MATH ESSENTIALS, 2 ed.
PRACTICAL SPELLING, 2 ed.
PRACTICAL VOCABULARY, 2 ed.
READ BETTER, REMEMBER MORE, 2 ed.
THE SECRETS OF TAKING ANY TEST, 2 ed.

Become a Better Student–*Quickly*
Become a More Marketable Employee–*Fast*
Get a Better Job–*Now*

HOW TO STUDY

HOW TO
STUDY
Second Edition

*Use Your Personal Learning Style to Help
You Succeed When It Counts*

by Gail Wood

LEARNINGEXPRESS
NEW YORK

Library of Congress Cataloging-in-Publication Data

Wood, Gail
    How to study : use your personal learning style to help you succeed when it counts / by
Gail Wood.
        p.   cm
    ISBN 1-57685-308-X (pbk.)
    1. Study skills. 2. Cognitive styles. 3. Learning.   I. Title.

    LB1049.W626 2000
    371.3'028'1—dc21

                                                                                        00-032720

Printed in the United States of America
9 8 7 6 5 4 3
First Edition

For Further Information
For information on LearningExpress, other LearningExpress products, or bulk sales,
please write to us at:
        LearningExpress®
        900 Broadway
        Suite 604
        New York, NY 10003

Or visit us at:
        www.learnatest.com

CONTENTS

INTRODUCTION

What do comfort and feeling good have to do with learning? Lots! When you have the right attitude and can focus on your studying in a style that's right for you, you learn more with seemingly less effort. In the 20 minutes a day that you'll spend with this book, you'll learn how to learn!

HOW TO USE THIS BOOK

To get the most out of studying, you need to find what works best for you. Other people can't tell you how to study. All they can do is to tell you what works for them. If you learn the same way as they do, their tips might be helpful. But if your style is different from theirs, those tips might not be very useful to you. In fact, they might even be a waste of your time.

GETTING COMFORTABLE WITH STUDYING

This book asks a lot of questions to help you learn how to study effectively. But there are no "right" or "wrong" answers here. Every question is designed to help you discover how *you* learn, and to help you do more of what works for you—whether you're reading a text, listening to a lecture, writing a paper, or preparing for a test.

For example, in order to understand what you're reading right now, you are doing something that works for you. Maybe you're reading this out loud. Or "hearing" your voice in your head as you read this silently. Perhaps you are making pictures on paper. Maybe you're reading this as you're walking. You might be reading all this in an orderly way, making a kind of outline in your head as you go along.

Each of these ways is a different learning style. And the early chapters in this book focus on helping you find your own learning style. Later chapters help you work with your learning style so you can use it more often. The icons shown to the left stand for the five learning styles you'll find out about in this book. Once you've identified your learning style in Chapter 2, "Discovering How You Learn," you can look in the later chapters for the icon that stands for your style to find study tips that will help you take advantage of your strength.

You're more comfortable when you're using your own style because you're understanding more. And when you're comfortable, you're more receptive—you find it easier to get involved with what you're studying, as you'll see in Chapter 9, "Getting Involved in Learning." When you're involved with what you're studying, it doesn't feel like work; it becomes something you enjoy.

Getting satisfaction from what you're studying requires careful planning. Dividing big jobs into little ones makes overwhelming tasks more bearable. There's a chapter in this book on that, too. Sometimes people can't pay close attention to their studying because something else needs to be done. Spending a few minutes on that other job before studying will ease the conscience—thus making studying more productive.

Also, some people work best if they work on several things at once. Maybe you've heard, "Can't you just do one thing at a time?" Well, for you perhaps the answer is, "No, I can't. I work best if I go back and forth between two or three projects. If I try to stick to one job at a time, I get distracted and don't work well." Many people work best this way. The trick is in paying close attention to yourself, in asking yourself, "When am I really focused? When am I feeling bored? When do I feel I'm "getting it"? When do I feel lost?" There are chapters here that help you use your learning style to understand and remember what you're reading or listening to.

At one time or another, everyone has dreaded the idea of studying for a particular exam, whether because the topic was extremely difficult or painfully boring. In such instances, studying with a partner might be the way to go. It's often easier and more enjoyable studying with someone else. The partner, or study buddy, can be a classmate, friend, coworker, or a family member. If your study buddy is studying the same topic you are, you can work as a team in developing questions and finding the answers. If your buddy is someone from outside class or work, she can act as your student as you teach her what you've been studying. Or she can act as your coach by asking you such questions as, "What part of this interested you most? Why? What sticks out in your mind?"

Once you've become more relaxed with the subject through working with a study buddy, you can work on your own, in a way that's similar to working with a partner. Later in this book, you'll find chapters about working with a study buddy and working on your own. It's all part of discovering what works best for you.

USING THIS BOOK IN 20 MINUTES A DAY

For most people, 20 minutes is just about the amount of time they can spend concentrating; then they need to take a break. That's why the chapters in this book are written so each one can be read in about 20 minutes. After 20 minutes, you may find your thoughts drifting, even if you're interested in the subject. If you stick to 20 minutes, you're apt to remember more, because you'll be concentrating the whole time. However, since everyone learns at his or her own pace, you might find that 20 minutes is too long. If you find your mind wandering before time is up, try working for 15 minutes at a time. If that's too long, try 10 minutes. Take a break for 10 or 15 minutes, and then return to your study.

Since everyone reads differently, the number of words or pages you can cover in 20 minutes may be more or less than one chapter of this book. That's OK. Just spend your 20 minutes (or less, depending on what works best for you) studying the material and going through the exercises, and don't worry about how much material you're covering. You're becoming your own teacher here. Your job is to find your pace. Give yourself the time it takes—whether you cover 20 lesson in 20 days, or 20 chapters in 40 days. Work with your own abilities and preferences so you can make the most of your time. The chapters are written in sequence, each one building on the ones that came before it. But that doesn't mean that you have to read them in this order. Look through the table of contents. Which chapter title interests you most? Try reading that one first. You want to get out of this book what *you* want to get out of it. Enjoy yourself as you learn!

Try It!

There are lots of activities and exercises in this book. Give yourself the time to do them. If this book belongs to you, you can write answers to some of the exercises right in it. But for some longer exercises—and for all the exercises if you borrowed this book from the library or from a friend—you'll need to write or draw on separate paper.

Find Out!

The symbols shown beside this paragraph are used in this book for such exercises. The best thing for you to do is to get a notebook that you can devote specifically to your notes and questions as you read along. Then you'll have a record of your answers and of your progress as you learn more about how you study.

NOTE: If you read the first edition of this book, you'll see some additions, and a few changes, in this, the second edition. In two years, there have been some changes in schools and in businesses.

- More and more students and workers speak a first language that's not English. What if English isn't your native language? This edition helps you become more comfortable and more fluent when using English in school, in the office, and at home.
- More and more schools and offices have computers—often requiring students and workers to use them. Whether it's your first time in front of a computer terminal, or you wish it were your last, this edition includes ways to use your learning styles to master the computer—and use it as a helpful tool to improve your study habits.

Also, for you to have a clearer sense of what kind of impact this book has on how you study, take the Test Your Study Smarts Survey that follows.

For an honest look at how understanding—and using—your learning styles can effect your studying, take this survey now, before you read this entire book, and take it again, after finishing the book. That way you can see any changes that might occur in the ways you study.

If this isn't your book, make sure you use a separate piece of paper to record your answers!

What's tricky is that if you don't know how you feel, or what you do or don't do, and just guess, the survey won't be accurate. It's important to spend some time thinking about how you really feel and what you really do—or don't do. O.K.? Ready? Let's go!

TEST YOUR STUDY SMARTS SURVEY

Circle the number that reflects how you feel, or the likeliness of what you do or don't do. There are no "right" or "wrong" answers. (Remember, it's important to think carefully and to respond accurately for the survey to work!)

As the numbers go up, it means the feeling, or likeliness, increases. Number 1 means "dread"—you feel awful. Number 2 means you're not dreading it, but you feel pretty uncomfortable. Number 3 means you feel a little uncomfortable. Number 4 is neutral—you don't care one way or the other. Number 5 means you feel a little comfortable, but not very much. Number 6 means you feel pretty comfortable. Number 7 means "delight"—you feel terrific, couldn't feel better.

For each question, think about being in a learning or studying situation, such as being in a class.

If you spoke another language before English, do this section first. If English is your first language, skip this section. Think about your feelings towards your *first* language, your "mother tongue."

How do you feel about reading?	1	2	3	4	5	6	7
How do you feel about listening?	1	2	3	4	5	6	7
How do you feel about writing?	1	2	3	4	5	6	7
How do you feel about speaking?	1	2	3	4	5	6	7

<u>In this section, think about how you feel using English.</u>

How do you feel about reading?	1	2	3	4	5	6	7
How do you feel about listening?	1	2	3	4	5	6	7
How do you feel about writing?	1	2	3	4	5	6	7
How do you feel about speaking?	1	2	3	4	5	6	7
How do you feel about math?	1	2	3	4	5	6	7
How do you feel about algebra?	1	2	3	4	5	6	7

<u>For this section, circle the answer that you feel applies to you now.</u>
Are you comfortable working with others?

Never   Rarely   Sometimes   Usually

Do you take notes (in writing or on cassette tape) while you read or listen?

Never   Rarely   Sometimes   Usually

Do you ask yourself questions as you read or listen?

Never   Rarely   Sometimes   Usually

Do you ask yourself questions as you write or calculate?

Never   Rarely   Sometimes   Usually

Do you make pictures in your head as you read or listen?

Never   Rarely   Sometimes   Usually

Do you make pictures in your head as you write or calculate?

Never   Rarely   Sometimes   Usually

Do you re-read what you've written?

Never   Rarely   Sometimes   Usually

Do you read what you've written out loud?

Never   Rarely   Sometimes   Usually

Note: Parts of this test are similar in concept to a student self-assessment questionnaire I developed a few years ago at the College of Staten Island, City University of New York, with Dr. Ivan Smodlaka, director of College Testing, and Dr. David Adams, who was then the director of Institutional Research at the College. We found that when students were more *comfortable* reading, writing, listening, and speaking—they got more out of what they studied. Students' grades increased more than students who did not feel more comfortable.

CHAPTER | 1

What do you do first? In order to get the most out of what you're studying, you need to be in the mood. It helps if you're relaxed and comfortable. It also helps if you're studying where, when, and how you like to work.

GETTING STARTED

A successful study session involves preparation. You have to get yourself ready so that you can get off to a good start. This means you've got to have all the things you need for the task and you need a good place to do it in. And maybe most important of all, you need to be mentally ready to begin. This lesson will help you find out how to get ready for productive study.

GETTING IN THE MOOD

You probably know what it's like to have to do something you don't feel like doing. Whether it's studying, washing the dinner dishes, or training a new person on the job, it's easy to put off doing an unpleasant task.

PROCRASTINATION

You can come up with plenty of excuses for not doing something:

- "I can't do the dishes now because I have to pay the bills."
- "I can't train Tony this morning because I'm expecting an important call."
- "I can't study now because I have to get a haircut."

At some time or another everyone *procrastinates*. The first step in conquering this problem is to recognize the actual reasons for procrastinating:

- You're not sure you can do it.
- You're afraid it will involve too much time and effort.
- You're uneasy in new situations.
- You don't want to be disturbed.
- It's hard for you to get started.

Knowing why you're procrastinating will help you overcome the tendency to put things off, and you'll find it easier to get moving.

Trick and Treat to Beat Procrastination

We all like be to rewarded for a job well done. And if we know there's going to be a reward at the end, we'll be more motivated at the start. You can apply this to studying: Trick yourself into working now by promising yourself a treat later.

 Before you read any further, think of a reward you can give yourself after you complete this lesson or before you begin the next one. Here are some suggestions for rewards to give yourself:

- Telephone a friend.
- Have a nutritious snack.
- Spend time with your pet: cat, dog, goldfish, hamster, hedgehog.
- Take a walk or exercise.

Next, take out a notebook and make a list of other rewards you'd like to give yourself–rewards that don't take a lot of time, aren't expensive, and are easy to do right where you are.

Use Procrastination to Get Something Done

Let the studying you *have* to do take turns with something else. Distract yourself from one job by doing the other. This works especially well if both tasks are the kind that make you want to procrastinate, like studying your psychology textbook and cleaning out your closet. Watch the clock; don't spend more than 20 minutes on one job. You can set a time less than 20 minutes if that works better for you—15 minutes, or even 10.

FINDING THE RIGHT CONDITIONS

To help you be at your best, you need to identify what helps you stay both alert and calm. Everyone is different, so it's important to get in touch with what works for *you*.

Dealing with Trouble

Josie is reluctant to sign up for a management course she needs to take to be considered for promotion. "I have so much trouble studying," she says, "I can't find the time. There are so many other things I have to do. And there's no place for me to study! I can't study at home because my brother's always playing the radio, and my neighbor's dog barks constantly."

If Josie can find the right study conditions for herself and make time in her schedule, she'll be on the road to becoming a manager.

WHAT WORKS FOR YOU

To help you get started finding your ideal study conditions, think about a project you completed. How did you feel before you began it, and how did you feel after finishing it? What did you do to get yourself started?

You might want to think about when you had something really important to do, such as gathering tax information or balancing your checkbook.

In your notebook, answer the following questions:

1. What time of day do you work best—morning, afternoon, or evening? How early or late in the day are you able to think clearly?
2. Do you prefer quiet, or do you need background music?
3. If you like background music, what kind?
4. Where do you like to work—at a desk, on a couch, on your bed?
5. What do you like to have around you when you work? Do you have a favorite pillow? A pet? Write whatever comes to mind. Remember, you're trying to get in touch with what helps keep you calm and alert.
6. What about eating—do you prefer working during or after a meal? What foods leave you feeling clear-headed and energized?

 The answers to these questions give you your ideal conditions. Read on to find out how you can make your ideal conditions when they don't occur naturally.

GETTING WHAT YOU NEED

Sometimes, the conditions of your ideal study situation just can't be met. Maybe you're a morning person, but you're at the office in the morning. Or, you're an evening thinker, but you work the night shift. What can you do? Of course, you can utilize the thinking time on days or nights when you're not working, but in order to make learning stick with you, it's a good idea to study each day, even if only for 20 minutes or so. You need to find time every day, not just on weekends.

Ask yourself: "What is it about my special time that helps me?" Write some ideas in your notebook. Then read on for ideas on how to plan your day to create your ideal study situation.

After a Rest

If your best study time is after a rest, then you're the kind of person who needs to work when you're refreshed. Try taking a nap before your study session. See if that helps. Or try going to bed earlier and waking up earlier. This way you could study *before* going to work or school.

When You're Relaxed

If you study better when you're really relaxed, like when you're in bed, put yourself to bed early!

Actually, reviewing something you want to remember for a half hour before you go to sleep and then re-reading the same material as soon as you wake up is a great way for anybody to study. Your brain is especially receptive then. Maybe you've had the experience of waking up in the middle of the night, suddenly remembering something, like "Tomorrow is my brother's birthday!" Such instances are spontaneous; you didn't plan to remember his birthday just then. But when you study upon waking, you're being deliberate; you're directing your brain to help you remember.

This technique can be used to come up with ideas and solve problems, too. Before going to sleep, try talking to yourself about an idea you want to come up with or a math problem that's presenting a challenge. Keep a pad of paper and a pencil by your bed so you'll be ready for the answers in the morning!

At a Desk

If you work best sitting at a desk, but you'd like to use your two-hour bus trip each day to study, re-create your desk on the bus! Buy a lap board from an office supply or art store. Glue a pencil case to a corner, so your tools will be easy to reach. Decorate the board with photos of favorite people or feel-good sayings you come across in magazines or fortune cookies—just make sure you leave the study area bare! If you need more light, try a miniature flashlight; some come in pens or on key chains. And make sure to take advantage of your real desk when you can.

With Background Noise

If you like noise around you, do a little study of yourself first. What kinds of music or TV make you comfortable? Keep in mind that the music you enjoy most might not work as background music for studying.

Read one section of this book with one kind of background sound, another section with another kind, and so on. Which section did you remember best? Some kinds of sounds, like TV or vigorous music, command your attention, making it difficult to focus on what you're studying.

The clue is to find what's comfortable so you get *the most out of studying*. You might find that soft classical music works best.

When It's Quiet

Do you think best in silence? Then you need to block out as much noise as you can. Get up early, go to bed late, study *after* the kids have gone to school. The rest of the time, create quiet: close the door to the living room, wear earplugs or headphones—or do anything you can to block out sounds.

Josie, from the box on page 3, might even be able to work something out with her brother. Maybe he would wear headphones so she could have quiet to study. Or maybe she could use headphones with music playing so softly that it wouldn't disturb her concentration but would still block out the noises around her.

Try different approaches to see what works for you. There are even machines you can buy that make *white noise* to block out distracting sounds. If you're thinking of buying one, make sure you hear it first. What works fine for one person might not work at all for another!

 In your notebook, make a list of alternate places to study, keeping in mind the best types of environments for you. Your local library is a good place to start!

KEEPING CALM

When you're calm, you can think clearly and deeply. You'll find it easier to make connections and to remember what you've been studying.

What Keeping Calm Can Do

Lenny freaked out when he saw the chemistry book: "I'm never going to get through that!" He felt so intimidated by the heavy book that he didn't open it until the day before the first quiz. But putting off studying only makes matters worse. If Lenny had spent time calming himself down, he could have opened the book the first time he saw it. He could have put himself in the mood and taken charge of his studying. He might even have become interested in chemistry!

PICTURE YOURSELF CALM

Think of a place that makes you feel calm. It can be a real place you've been to, some place you've seen in a movie or photograph, or a fantasy place you made up. Close your eyes and get a clear picture of this place in your head. Try to imagine yourself really there. Sense what you see, hear, feel, and smell.

For example, if you're imagining yourself on a beach . . .

- See yourself sitting on the shore.
- Hear the gentle waves lapping the shore and an occasional seagull calling.
- Feel the warm sand on your toes and the gentle breeze on your shoulders.
- Smell the salt water.

By using your four senses in this imagination exercise, rather than just one or two, you heighten the sensation of peace and relaxation, making a mental image seem like reality.

AS EASY AS BREATHING

Another exercise you can do to become calm is deep breathing. You may want to first put your mind in your special imaginary place.

- Listen to one of the sounds in your special place, perhaps the gentle waves lapping the shore. Put your hand over your heart and listen to your heartbeat.
- With this sound in your head, and sitting comfortably with your back straight, breathe in, feeling your chest fill with air.
- Breathe out, feeling the emptiness in your chest.
- Repeat breathing in and out several times, inhaling and exhaling, feeling calmer each time you breathe out.

Use this technique when you feel stressed—because of an upcoming exam, an enormous chemistry book, or a looming deadline—and you'll feel more relaxed and ready to begin.

IN SHORT

Keeping calm helps you remain clear-headed. Rewarding yourself, before and/or after studying helps you get in the mood. Working only for as long as you can stay alert and pay attention—20 minutes at a time for most people—helps keep you in the studying mood. Studying in a favorite place, at a time of day when you're at your thinking best, helps you make the most of your study time and efforts.

Practice Tips

Here are some ways you can practice the suggestions of this chapter in everyday situations. Doing so will make you feel experienced and more comfortable when you use these same methods to get started studying.

- The next time you find yourself feeling anxious at work or at home, try imagining a special place and practice deep breathing to calm yourself.
- The next time you find yourself not wanting to do something that needs to be done, reward yourself before and/or after doing the task.
- Before doing something you've never done, do something familiar that you can easily accomplish in a short period of time.
- Before doing something new, review what you have done that's similar.

CHAPTER 2

You like surprises and your friend Harry hates them. You love movies, but Harry would rather listen to music. You like different things because you think differently. You and Harry will probably get more out of studying if you combine your different styles.

DISCOVERING HOW YOU LEARN

Suppose you and your friend Harry are in an American history class, studying the events that led up to World War I. Films and tapes of speeches about the period are in the school library. Since you love movies, you might get more out of watching the films. Since Harry prefers listening, he might get more out of listening to speeches. If you were to just listen to the speeches and Harry were to watch the films, neither of you would fully understand what you're studying.

PEOPLE THINK AND LEARN DIFFERENTLY

How do *you* learn? We all have two eyes, two ears, a nose, but we each look unique. People aren't the same on the outside, and they're not the same inside either. Everyone has their own *learning style*. You were born with yours and Harry was born with his; different parts of everybody's brain are—well, different!

Think of a person as a seesaw. It's pretty unusual for someone to be a perfectly level seesaw, with all learning styles having the same strength, or weight. For most of us, the seesaw is tilted. Where it goes up, we have more learning strength, and where it goes down, we have less. We tilt one way or another but we all stay in the air because one side compensates for the other. It's important to know how you learn best, so you can do more of what works best for you.

You can find clues about how you learn best by looking for a similarity in the things you like to do. You learn in many different ways, and you have your own *combinations of learning styles*. Usually, you're comfortable doing certain activities and you get more out of these activities because they match your learning styles.

The purpose of this chapter is to help you get in touch with the styles with which you're most comfortable. Once you've identified these styles, you can move on to the later chapters that focus on a specific style of learning.

FIVE LEARNING STYLES

There are five different learning styles. Most people have at least one dominant style, but everyone uses a combination of learning styles, sometimes depending on the activity they're doing.

- **Eyes.** If you like to watch movies and draw or paint, or get involved in other activities that rely on your eyes, you are probably a *visual learner*. Visual learners mainly use their eyes to learn.

- **Ears.** If you'd rather listen to the radio than read the paper, if you like listening to music and/or lectures, or participate in other activities that depend on your ears, you are probably an *auditory learner*. Auditory learners mostly use their ears to learn.

- **Order.** If you like to do crossword puzzles, fill out forms, work math problems, or do other activities in an orderly way, you are probably a *sequential learner*. Sequential learners need to put things in a particular order so they can learn them.

- **Images.** If you make pictures or designs in your head as you're looking at or listening to something, you are learning through *images*. People who learn through images are usually *global learners*. These people like to see the whole picture and often don't need to work through individual parts, as sequential learners do.

- **Doing.** If you like to keep moving—whether it's the big-movement action of sports or dancing, or a small-movement action such as doodling, playing an instrument, or needlework, you might learn best by motion, and be a *kinesthetic learner*. Kinesthetic learners learn best when they keep their bodies or hands moving.

GET IN TOUCH WITH YOUR STYLE

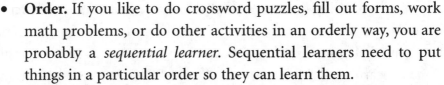

Here's an activity using five general styles to help you get in touch with how you learn.

- Write in your notebook a list of things you like to do, and things you're good at. Include the kinds of jobs you enjoy, clubs you belong to or to which you'd like to belong, and things you haven't done but wish you could.
- Make five columns, one for each general learning style: eyes, ears, order, images, and doing.
- Now take each item from your list and put it in the appropriate column. Some things might appear in more than one column. For instance, playing the clarinet could be both *doing* (the fingers are doing the walking) and *ears* (listening).
- Add the number of items in each column. Which columns have the most? These are the ones that most likely represent your strongest learning styles.

You'll probably find ways other than these five that are particularly helpful to you. What's important is that you keep looking for connections between what you do and how you do it. There are as many combinations of learning styles as there are people! The way to find out about yourself is to pay close attention to *when and how* you pay close attention.

HOW DO YOU REMEMBER?

The next time someone gives you a phone number, pay attention to what you do to try to remember the number. Write in your notebook what you do.

 Do you see the numbers in your head?

 Do you say the numbers, perhaps over and over, in your head?

 Do you do both?

 Do you write the numbers in the air with your finger?

 Do you make a picture of the numbers in your head?

Do you hear the tones of the numbers in your head?

 Do you put the numbers in certain groupings?

12

RIGHT-BRAIN VERSUS LEFT-BRAIN THINKING

Another kind of difference in learning styles has to do with whether the right side or the left side of your brain is dominant. Your brain hemispheres crisscross to your hands. This means that if you're left-handed, the right side of your brain is probably more developed. If you're right-handed, you probably rely on the left side of your brain more than the right. Each side has its own jobs to do, although the two sides do communicate with each other. You might find traits of how you think in both sides.

Right-brain thinkers (who are usually left-handed) tend to be creative types. They are good at coming up with new ideas. Many artists, poets, and composers are right-brain thinkers.

Left-brain thinkers (who are usually right-handed) are more orderly in their thought processes. There are many more left-brain thinkers than right-brain thinkers, so you'll find left-brain thinkers in all kinds of occupations.

Each kind of thinking has its own strengths. While the right-brain thinker will come up with a good idea for the theme of a birthday party, the left-brain thinker is the one you would want to count on to organize the party: send out the invitations, get the food, and find people to help decorate. The right-brain thinker will be good at creative games like charades, while the left-brain thinker will be good at games that require logic and following rules, like checkers or bridge. The right-brain thinker loves to dance and may even make up new steps to go with the music. The left-brain thinker may like to dance, too, because he or she will find it easy to learn the steps of the waltz, mambo, or electric slide. Right-brain thinkers like the rhythm of poetry. Left-brain thinkers like figuring out the meaning of a poem.

As you'll see in the next section, it matters whether you're a right-brain or a left-brain thinker because each kind of thinking requires different kinds of study habits.

So what's your next step? To find out what kind of thinker you are!

RIGHT OR LEFT?

Are you left-handed (right brain) or right-handed (left brain)? This will give you a clue, but a lot of left-handed people have some left-brain tendencies, and right-handed people may have right-brain tendencies. So try this exercise to see where you fall.

- **Go back to the list** of favorite things you made in the exercise earlier in this chapter.
- **Circle** any items that have to do with rhythm, music, art, or creative thinking.
- **Underline** any items that have to do with solving a problem, organizing something, or thinking logically.

Your circles are connected with right-brain thinking. Your underlines are connected with left-brain thinking. Which do you have more of?

STUDY TIPS FOR LEFT-BRAIN THINKERS

If in the exercise above you had more underlines than circles, then you're probably more comfortable with logical and abstract ways of relating to the world around you.

Logical Thinking

You have a structured, organized way of thinking. Concepts called *syllogisms*, like, "If A = B, and B = C, then A = C" come easily to you.

If this is you, here are some ways you can use your left-brain strengths in studying:

- **Find similarities.** Look for connections within or between the topics you're studying. For example: words that look or sound alike, laws made for similar reasons or that have similar impact.
- **Write or record** what makes them similar in your notebook or on tape.
- **Ask yourself** what the similarities could mean. Write or record your answers.
- **Use numbers** in writing or speaking to classify the importance of the similarities.

Abstract Thinking

You don't always want to know exactly what something is because you prefer to figure it out yourself. You like algebra better than arithmetic. The meanings in short stories, novels, or poems come easily to you.

If this is you:

- **Begin in the middle**—whether you're reading a text, reviewing your notebook, or listening to taped notes.
- **Write or record what you know for sure** and what questions come to mind. Use symbols. For example, if you're studying monarchies in history class, you could draw a crown in the margin of your notebook. Use colors, or different intonations in a recording, to help you remember the connections between your questions and the topics you know for sure.
- **Search the text or taped recording for your answers,** then write them down or record them.
- **Write or record a summary** using your symbols, colors, or intonations.

STUDY TIPS FOR RIGHT-BRAIN THINKERS

If in the exercise above you had more circles than underlines, you're probably more comfortable with literal and creative ways of relating to the world around you.

Literal Thinking

You need to see something to be convinced. You may prefer math and geometry to algebra, and non-fiction to short stories and novels.

If this is you, here are some ways you can use your right-brain strengths in studying:

- **Remind yourself of what you know for sure.** Check illustrations and charts carefully before, during, and after you read. If there aren't any in the text, make them!
- **Choose and use colors** to identify characters or themes in a story, and different procedures in algebra or math (for example: green could be adding; red, subtracting; black, multiplying; and so on).

Creative Thinking

If you're a right-brain thinker, you're probably pretty good at coming up with ideas.

If this is you:

- **Use your imagination.** Pretend the text is a speech or a play and you're the announcer or actor. Come up with your own ideas on this!

Rhythm

Musical rhythms, songs, or the beats in poetry come easily to you.

If this is you:

- **Tap your foot or fingers** as you read your text as if it were a song or poem. This works with numbers, too.

Art

You like to look at or make drawings, sculptures, or paintings.

If this is you:

- **Draw pictures** of what something you're reading means to you. Turn the text into your own cartoon.

You've come a long way already. Now you know which side of the brain dominates your thinking and you have used that knowledge to find learning styles that will help you learn more efficiently. In the next three chapters, you'll be exploring those styles, one by one.

WHAT IF ENGLISH ISN'T YOUR FIRST LANGUAGE?

O.K. Now you have a general idea of what your learning styles are. But you spoke another language before you learned English. Reading in English takes a little longer than reading in your native language. Some native English speakers talk a little too fast for you to understand them. What can you do?

The trickiest part of learning a new language is the simplest. *CLOSE YOUR EYES.* Let your ears do the work. No matter what kind of a learner you are, you learned your native language by listening. That's why a native language is sometimes called a "mother tongue," because the first sounds a baby hears, the first words a baby hears, are usually from the mother.

Do you like to watch television? Close your eyes. Let your ears do the work of understanding what's happening. It can be easy to figure out what is happening just by looking.

- If you learn best by hearing, maybe you are already comfortable speaking—and listening—to English. Maybe you are more concerned with reading, and writing, in English.
- If you learn best by seeing, maybe you are more comfortable reading English than you are speaking it. Maybe you are more concerned with speaking in English.

SEEING + HEARING = UNDERSTANDING

The more you see and hear English at the same time, the more readily you'll be able to read and write in English! Check out your school or local library for subtitled films. When you see the words you're hearing, you'll become more familiar with them. (Occasionally, a sentence is written in subtitles shorter than it's spoken on the screen. When this is done, the meaning remains the same.) You may be able to get close-captioning—subtitles embedded in the broadcast signal—for your home television, too.

The more you speak English, the easier it is to write it. By being familiar with the way English sounds, we know where words and punctuation marks go. Punctuation is based on where we pause (comma) and where we stop (period) when we speak. How can you put yourself in situations where you'll speak English more often? Look into clubs at school or in your neighborhood, where people with a similar hobby or interest get together. And, remember to have fun!

IN SHORT

You learn from your eyes, ears, by making images, by putting ideas in order, and by doing. You have your own combination of learning styles. Things you like to do for fun, and the ways you do them, can help show you what your learning styles are. And, as you know by now, you get more out of studying when you use the ways you learn best.

Practice Tips

Think back, then write the answers to these questions in your notebook.

- Who were your favorite teachers?
- How did your favorite teachers address your learning style?
- What did they do to help you learn?

CHAPTER | 3

The eyes have it—and so
do the ears. These are the
two most common study
styles. Is one of them your
strongest? Whether you
answer yes or no, you
probably use both
styles often. In this chapter,
you'll learn how to make
the most of what you see
and what you hear.

LOOKING AND LISTENING

In Chapter 2, you began to discover your own learning styles by looking at what you like to do and what comes to you easily. You looked at five different styles, and you probably found that one or two of them are most important to you. This chapter concentrates on two of those styles: using your eyes and using your ears. Most people find that they rely heavily on one or the other of these–even people who also rely on images, order, or doing to help them learn.

EYES OR EARS

Few people actively use *both* their eyes and their ears in learning new things. One or the other is usually much stronger. In this chapter, you'll continue to explore whether you are more a visual or an auditory learner. Once you've done that, you'll learn study tips that will help you take advantage of your strength and help you learn to use the weaker learning style. After all, you sometimes *have* to use a style that's not your strongest. If you're listening to a tape or a lecture, you have to use your ears, whether you're an auditory learner or not. If you're reading or making an observation, your eyes play the lead role, whether you're a visual learner or not. So while you can learn to take advantage of your strong side, you have to learn to use your weaker side as well.

In this chapter, you'll find out how to make more of seeing and hearing–both by using your own learning strength, and by finding ways to work within a situation that doesn't cater to your predominant style.

Matching the Situation with Your Learning Style

Jonah and Mike are both studying Public Speaking. Jonah learns better by hearing, and Mike learns better by seeing. When responding to speeches by classmates, Jonah listens carefully, giving the speaker his full attention, and Mike tries to write as much as he hears, underlining what's important or interesting to him. Mike also pays attention to visual aids, such the blackboard or handouts. Both Jonah and Mike give similar responses to the speaker, but they have to focus on the speech in very different ways. If Jonah just wrote notes, and Mike just listened, they both would have a problem understanding what the speech was about.

DO YOU SEE OR HEAR BETTER?

Imagine running into a friend you haven't seen for a long time. The friend is in a hurry to catch a bus. Neither one of you has paper or pen. The friend tells you his phone number. What do you do to try to remember the number?

Imagine you're traveling by bus to a town you haven't been to before. You pass a billboard with important hotel and restaurant information. You don't have paper and pen with you. What do you do to try to remember what's on the billboard?

Which exercise above came more naturally to you?

- Was it the phone exercise? If so, you probably learn better by hearing.
- Was it the billboard exercise? Then you probably learn better by seeing.
- Were the two exercises the same for you? Yes? Then you probably learn better when you see and hear something at the same time.

BOOST YOUR EYE OR EAR POWER

OK, now that you know whether you learn better with your ears or your eyes, what do you do to study more effectively? Whether you're summarizing what you read, or reflecting on what happened in the last class, try one of these techniques:

- Give yourself something to hear: speak! Take notes by speaking into a tape recorder. You can play this back not only at your best study time (see Chapter 1), but in a headset when you're commuting to or from work, when you're on your lunch hour, doing dishes at home, or going for a walk.

- Give yourself something to see: write or draw! Carry a little notebook or sketch pad around with you to write or draw afterthoughts of what you studied. You can study not only at your best time of day, but since you're carrying your notes with you, whenever you have a few minutes–even in the bathtub.

BE ALL EARS

Here are ways to make the most of using your ears in studying, whether they're your learning strength or not.

WHEN LISTENING

Use only your ears. Try closing your eyes when you're listening to something you want to remember, whether it's a tape of a speech or notes you taped into a recorder. Now your ears have to do all the work! Try the same thing when you're on the phone or listening to news on the radio or TV. Closing your eyes can help your ears focus. You're helping your ears get the most out of what you hear by not letting what you see get in the way.

Learning a New Language?

If you're studying a language, the sooner your ear becomes familiar with the sound and rhythms of that language, the easier it will be for you to use that language, both in speaking and writing. Tune into the language you're learning by listening to radio talk shows and TV programs in that language. Remember to close your eyes! You're *just* using your ears. It's too easy for your eyes to figure out what's happening on TV.

WHEN READING

When you're reading something you want to remember, try reading out loud. Listen to your voice and change the sound of it when the mood of what you're reading changes. Have fun making deep and high sounds, loud and soft sounds. Have you ever noticed in a play or movie, that just before actors say something important, like, "The butler did it," they pause? There's usually a pause after they say it as well. Decide what's important to you in what you're reading, and try pausing before and after you say that. Try it right now with this paragraph.

IT'S IN THE EYES

Here are ways to make the most of using your eyes in studying, whether they're your learning strength or not.

WHEN LISTENING

When you're listening to something you want to remember, try drawing a picture or taking notes. If you're drawing, draw what comes to mind right away. These are your notes, so they have to make sense to *you!* Stick figures are fine. If you're writing, pretend you're a newspaper reporter with a lot of readers. It'll help you focus on what's important, and your notes will be clearer to you if you pretend you're writing them for someone else.

WHEN READING

When you're reading something you want to remember, draw or write. If you're writing, try choosing the most important word in a sentence, then the most important sentence in the paragraph. Underline it if it's your own book; if it's not, write it in your notebook. Explain why it's important; summarize what you read in words. If you're drawing, make a series of pictures, just like in a comic strip, summarizing what sticks out in your mind about what you read.

STRENGTHEN YOUR EYES AND EARS

Practice focusing on looking and listening when watching TV.

- **Use your ears.** Close your eyes. Talk (even to yourself!) about what you heard.

- **Use your eyes.** Turn off the sound. Draw or write about what you saw.

Write in your notebook about what using your ears and then your eyes was like for you. Thinking back to what you heard or saw, what sticks out in your mind? Which was easier, relying on your eyes or your ears? What did you need to do in order to concentrate when using your less-favored style? The answer to this question can help you build up your eyes if you learn better by hearing, and build up your ears if you learn better by seeing.

If seeing or hearing is a problem for you, fast-forward to Chapter 20, "Knowing When You Need Help."

In Short

Discover whether you learn better by seeing, hearing, or both, by paying close attention to what you do and how you do it. Make the most of studying by doing it in the style you do best. If you learn better by seeing, write or draw summaries and reflections. If you learn better by hearing, talk and read out loud; tape your own notes, if possible. You can also strengthen how you hear or how you see by focusing just on sound or sight.

Practice Tips

If you learn better by hearing, say out loud what was useful to you in this chapter. If you learn better by seeing, write or draw a cartoon about it.

Here are some other ways to build up your seeing and hearing:

- See more: Check with your local or school library on viewing *closed-caption films*. These films show you what is being said by having the words appear on the bottom of the screen.
- Hear more: Check with your local or school library for books on tape. Just about every kind of book is available.

If you learn better when you combine seeing with hearing, write or draw what was useful, then read it aloud, or describe the drawing out loud.

CHAPTER | 4

MAKING IMAGES, MAKING ORDER, MAKING SENSE

As you study, your mind naturally creates images of what you're learning, and puts what you're hearing or seeing into some kind of order. Information makes more sense to us when both the pictures in our mind and the sequence of events are clear. Some of us learn by using lots of images. And some of us are strong sequential learners. This chapter will show you how to build on both strengths.

Think of a time when you and a friend were discussing a movie you both saw. You might have said something like, "Did you *see* the *time* he walked down the stairs and came to a mirror?" Maybe your friend answered, "Do you mean the time he saw the pianist?" Wait a minute: Can you *see* a *time*? Of course not; an image is one thing and the order of things is something else. But there is a connection. A movie is a set of moving pictures in a certain order. You make sense of a movie when you get involved with pictures, *and* follow the order of events. Similarly, you make sense of what you're studying if you can make an image of it *and* put it in order.

Understanding imagery and order makes what you're studying clearer to you. Even figuring out a math problem is something you do in different ways. The problem "5 x 2" has a lot more meaning if you "see" five branches of a pear tree with two pears on each branch. You use order in solving that same problem by putting ("seeing") the two groups of five together to make ten.

You may be someone who thinks best by putting things in order (a sequential thinker), or by using images (a global thinker). But even if those aren't your strengths, almost everything you study requires *some* images and *some* order, and you'll be a better learner by strengthening these styles.

TIPS FOR EVERYONE ON IMAGES AND ORDER
USING IMAGERY

The concrete world is made up of images. But not everyone can use their senses to "see" images in a book or on a tape. To know if you're really understanding the imagery of what you're reading or listening to, draw a map or a picture of what you see or hear. Is your image complete? If it's vague or missing something, you may need more information. If so, go back to the text or tape again.

USING ORDER

Order is the result of connections; if you discover connections between different events or facts, you'll most likely be able to put them in some sort of order. To know if you're understanding the order of what you're reading or listening to, make a list of events and number them in the order they occur. Or make a timeline: draw a line and write in or draw events in the order they occur. If you need more information to complete your list or timeline, review the text or audiotape.

Seeing Images vs. Seeing Order

Lilly and Amelia work together as paralegals. They just started a pre-law program at their local college.

In her office cubicle, Lilly has her files arranged around her in open wire baskets of different colors. Lilly is an *image* thinker; she can only learn something if she can picture it in her head. She associates images with other images in a comprehensive way that doesn't follow a specific order. This way of thinking is also called global thinking. When writing a paper, Lilly begins by drawing a picture of what she wants to say or imagining the picture in her head. Lilly needs to hold on to the images in her head that produce her ideas.

Amelia's files are kept in drawers in both alphabetical and numerical order. Amelia can only learn something effectively if she can understand an order, or sequence, to it. Amelia is a sequential learner. She begins her paper by writing an outline. She might change the outline somewhat as the paper progresses, but she needs to work with her sense of order.

If Lilly were required to make an outline, and Amelia to draw a picture, they probably would not get as much out of writing the paper as if their styles were reversed.

ARE YOU AN IMAGE THINKER OR A SEQUENTIAL THINKER?

IMAGE THINKERS

How can you tell if you think best by imagining things in pictures? Answer the following questions and find out.

- Do you remember people's faces well?
- If you leave bills or receipts in different places, do you usually remember where they are?
- When watching a sports event, do you usually see in your head what might happen next?

- Do you usually like to fuss with the way something is arranged, such as furniture or flowers?
- Are you apt to notice if a picture is not hung straight?

If you answered yes to at least three of the above, you probably think in images. You learn more powerfully by the pictures you see in your mind.

SEQUENTIAL THINKERS

How can you tell if you think best by putting an order to things? Answer the following questions and find out:

- Is it easy for you to be on time for an appointment?
- Do you like to do crossword puzzles?
- Do your friends or family tell you you're good at filling out forms?
- Do you file bills or receipts you want to save in a certain order?
- Does your watch have the actual time?

If you answered yes to at least three of the above, you're probably a strong sequential thinker. You just naturally seem to know the order of things.

Or, maybe in some ways you learn sequentially, and in other ways you learn globally, with images. Only *you* learn like *you*.

TIPS FOR IMAGE THINKERS

Lilly and Amelia like studying together. Lilly relates what she's studying to what she already knows in very broad ways, often in ways that would not occur to Amelia. Lilly is what's called a *global thinker*.

When Lilly is trying to understand a text that focuses on order, she uses imagery to help her understand the order of events. History class was a challenge for her. "All those dates!" she exclaimed. "They don't make sense to me." She focused on the pictures that came to mind first. Then, she put the pictures in an order, like making a cartoon. She associated dates with the pictures. She used imagery to understand the order of events.

Here are some tips to help you if you learn best by thinking in images:

- **To make the most of reading:** Take notes by drawing pictures that come to mind or describing the pictures in your head into a tape recorder.
- **To make the most of writing:** Describe the pictures in your head on paper or into a recorder, and then write what you play back.

```
1.
2.
3.
```

TIPS FOR SEQUENTIAL THINKERS

Amelia sees connections in an order that might be based on time or importance. In either case, she naturally thinks in an orderly way. Amelia is what's called a *sequential thinker*. She notes events and puts them in a sequence to understand them.

When Amelia is trying to understand a text that focuses on imagery, she uses her sense of order. Her poetry class was a challenge—all those descriptions! She turned her reading into a kind of detective story, asking herself: "What happened first? Then what happened? What next? What led up to the ending?" It was her sense of sequence that allowed her to create pictures in her head of what happened.

If you learn best by thinking in order:

- **To make the most of reading:** Write and re-write your notes in list or outline form, putting details under major topic headings. If you're using a tape recorder, read your list into it. As you play it back, listen to any changes you want to make so that the order is clearer or stronger for you.
- **To make the most of writing:** List or outline what you want to say. Your outline might be a series of questions. If so, put similar questions together to form categories. If you're using a tape recorder to get started, read your questions into it, play it back and re-record any changes that make the order clearer to you.

IN SHORT

There are two general ways to make sense of what you're studying:

1. Understand the imagery of what you've read or heard. Make pictures in your head. Go back to the text for information to make the pictures clearer.
2. Understand the order in what you've read or heard. Number events or make a timeline that shows you the order of events.

If you're a global thinker, you think more in pictures and make connections that don't necessarily follow a certain order. If you're a sequential thinker, your connections are based on time or importance.

Practice Tips

Use imagery *and* order the next time you study. After you read, draw what pictures come to mind. Then, go back and number events as they occur—on the text, if it's yours, in your notebook if it's not. Make a timeline of the events. Go back to the text for any information you need to make your picture and timeline clearer.

CHAPTER | 5

When you experience something first-hand, you're a more active learner than when you just watch or listen to someone else's experience. Also, being involved in an activity can trigger thinking. Some people learn better when they're doing something or when a part of them is moving; these people are kinesthetic learners. This chapter shows you how active learning is important, no matter what your learning style. It also shows you how to use movement and doing to study more effectively.

LEARNING BY DOING

How did you learn to ride a bike? To dance? To speak? You learned by doing. Nothing can replace the physical act of doing the thing you're trying to learn. Participating in a dance class forces the dancer to *experience* the movements she is trying to learn, thereby accelerating her learning process. Passively watching a dance recital may help her decide what kind of expertise she wants to acquire; however, she will not become an accomplished dancer by simply observing.

Everyone needs to use techniques of active learning to some extent to supplement their unique learning style. And if you found in Chapter 2, "Discovering How You Learn," that you learn primarily by doing, by kinesthetic learning, you need to see how you can maximize this style in your studying.

BECOMING AN ACTIVE LEARNER

When you're an active learner, you feel more in control of your studying. You're actively using *your* questions, *your* answers, *your* images, *your* order. You're noting what's important to *you*. You'll find you *want* to study when you're making these decisions for yourself. Assume responsibility for your own learning, and learning will become enjoyable.

One way to be an active learner is to think ahead before you read something.

 Right now, write the answers to these questions in your notebook, or speak them into your tape recorder.

- What are you expecting to happen in this chapter?
- What questions do you have about this chapter?

Use It and You'll Learn It!

Tom was not very interested in his Spanish class. Then he met Claudio, a new neighbor who had recently arrived from Puerto Rico. Claudio knew some English, but not enough to shop for groceries, so Tom offered to take him shopping. Tom was surprised at what he remembered from Spanish class as he explained different foods to Claudio in the grocery store. When Claudio responded in Spanish, Tom was often able to figure out new words because he was using language in a meaningful way—he was *experiencing* Spanish. It was then that Tom's attitude toward Spanish changed. He began to look forward to each class, because at home he was *using and learning* Spanish.

PLAY THE PART YOU WANT TO BE

One way to be an active learner is to *act the part* of a learner. By doing so, you will feel more in control of your studying. Here are a few ways you can role play and become an active learner:

- Pretend you're the instructor. Decide what you want the class (you) to focus on.
- Choose a character from the material you're studying, and pretend you are that character. If there's dialogue in the text, this is an especially effective exercise. If you're listening to a tape of a speech, pretend you're the speaker. What part of your speech did you like best? If you're reading a biography, take the part of that person and try to imagine what it would be like to live that life.
- Create a character. Perhaps you're studying a text without any characters—biology, for example. You could be a laboratory technician, comparing cell samples. Or an anthropologist, preparing to study animals in their natural habitat. Or an ecologist, studying native fauna or flora to reconstruct a preserved woodlands. The possibilities are endless.
- Talk to yourself as you imagine the character would, based on what you remember from the tape or reading.
- If you're working with a study buddy, you can each be a different character, and discuss—or argue about!—the topic you're studying. (You may want to skip ahead to Chapter 16, "Working with a Study Buddy," for some ideas.)

WATCHING CAN BE LIKE DOING

Think of a time when you were watching a sports event. Maybe it was a football or baseball game, or a hockey match. How did you get involved in that game? Maybe you jumped up when a certain play was made. Why? Did you shout out? Did you feel your stomach tighten or your heart pound at a suspenseful moment? Even though you were a spectator, watching someone else's experience, you were still *experiencing* the game. And you can do that in studying.

MAKE THINGS HAPPEN

When you are learning certain skills, it helps to be in the actual place you'd use those skills, like a lab, a police station, a nursery school, or a health clinic. But this isn't always possible. For instance, if you were learning to fly a plane, you'd first spend time in a simulator, a computerized cockpit on the ground that simulates flying. Another option is to use your imagination to visualize yourself in an actual situation, in an actual place. Involve yourself with the material by asking *your own questions,* in addition to any assigned questions, and then finding your own answers. You become an active learner when you *create your own experience.*

Move Around to Refresh and Re-focus

Larry was so nervous about a civil service test coming up that his brain would freeze whenever he tried to study. He would open his book, and although he knew what the words meant, he just couldn't put them together. He sat there trying to study, but nothing seemed to make sense. All the while, he was thinking of how important the test was and how he had to get a good grade. In frustration, he got up and went for a walk for half an hour. Then a strange thing happened. The more he walked, the clearer his head felt. After awhile, he found himself thinking about what he had been trying to study. When he returned to his book, the words made sense for the first time.

SUGGESTIONS FOR KINESTHETIC LEARNERS

If using your body or hands is the primary way you learn, there are several ways you can make the most of your learning style.

WALK AS YOU READ OR WRITE

Whether outside on a warm day or through the hallways of your home or library, you'll find this technique a good way to make sense of difficult reading or to overcome writer's block. If doing is your style, you may find ideas just popping into your head as you walk!

Use a Computer

If you don't own a computer, ask around at school, work, or the local library for one you can use. You'll find it's almost like having a study buddy. There's constant action involved when using a computer. Your hands are moving back and forth on the keyboard and, if you have a mouse, you're pushing it around the mouse pad. The screen, too, is always in motion. The cursor skips across the window; words and images scroll up and down. The quick response on the screen as you push a key or click a mouse button can make studying a more stimulating experience.

It can make studying a more magical experience, too. Press a button on the keyboard and you have a file cabinet, fancy typewriter, calculator, secretary, post office, and library.

If English is your second language, use a larger-size type font, and double- or triple-space whatever you're working on. It's easier to recognize a foreign language, especially a foreign alphabet, if it's set larger. If you're turning in a paper at school or work, you may need to reduce the size of the font—but keep the larger size for yourself. Remember, too, to read out loud (even if you're a visual learner!) to check if what you've written sounds like standard English.

New to the computer?

There are folks who can introduce you. If you're about to use a computer at school or work, trained staff are generally available to help you. If you bought a home computer, chances are that the manual that came with it has a phone number to call if you have questions.

- If the computer in general is making you nervous, try making it friendlier, more familiar. Put something you like on or near it. (As long as it's not edible! If food or drink seeps into the computer, it can interfere with what the computer is trying to do.) Maybe you have a favorite postcard or photograph. Maybe you have an unbreakable miniature figure or statue of a favorite animal, a totem, or icon. You choose! The idea is to help make the unfamiliar familiar.

- If it's typing on the computer, facing that blank screen, that gives you the heebee-jeebies, turn the monitor light down. (The dial is usually under the monitor. It may have symbols such as a sun at one end and moon at the other, for lightening and darkening your screen.) Everything you type will still register; you just won't be seeing it. Try it. Remember to continue to press SAVE as you're typing. When you feel calmer, turn the screen back on. You may find you wrote more than usual. Remember to keep writing until you've answered your questions, created clear pictures, and presented your thoughts in an order that makes sense to you. Save correcting for last! (You may want to take a sneak-peek at Chapter 19, Preparing for Essay Tests, for more suggestions on writing and editing.)

E-Mail

Some people become so attached to sending and receiving e-mail messages, they refer to "regular" letters as being "snail-mail." Even people who say they don't like to write enjoy sending e-mail messages.

What's tricky is to make sure you have the *exact* e-mail address of the person you're sending a message to. Make sure each letter, number, and symbol is accurate. It's important, too, to use the same kind of spacing, or lack of spacing! The computer does what you tell it to. Exactly. Every punctuation mark, every space, each letter needs to be in the same precise order of the person's e-mail address.

What's easy is that to answer someone's e-mail, you click onto REPLY. Then, simply confirm that it's going to the person who sent you a message. In addition, you can print a copy, and the initial message can be repeated in your reply.

Some schools, libraries, and offices offer free courses for students and employees to learn how to use computers. Check it out!

The Internet

The Internet is a gigantic network that behaves something like telephone lines. Anyone with an Internet link can click on to a source such as an online library. There is so much information available on the Internet—even translations of documents that previously were very difficult to obtain—that some libraries are focussing on Internet collections for library-users to use.

If the Personal Computer Is Old Hat to You

Discover new ways to use the computer in studying. For example, e-mail can be a boon to working with a study buddy. Even if both you and your buddy have tight schedules and find it difficult to arrange meeting times with each other, e-mail is something you can read or send at any time. Make sure you keep a copy of your message! What's fresh in the mind one day, can become confusing another day.

E-MAIL YOURSELF. It's a simple way to

—remind yourself of something you want to do

—draft a paper you're working on

—draft an e-mail message that you want to review later.

Computer Reminders

- Save everything! When writing, drawing, doing math calculations, or composing a long e-mail message on the computer, create a file to save what you're working on. With some computers, go to the word "file" and click on "save as." Type in the name and/or date you want to call the file. As you continue working, click "save" from time to time to keep what you've done—perhaps after a page or sooner. This is important because a file could be accidentally closed by an electrical malfunction, accidentally touching a key, or mistakenly pressing a combination of keys.

- Computers run on electricity or batteries. If yours plugs in, get a surge protector to safe-guard the system if there's an inconsistent electric current that may erase what you're working on.

- Make sure you're sitting comfortably, in an ergonomically sound chair, with feet flat on the floor, and supports for your wrists. Or, prop your feet on a stool. Wrist supports help prevent tendonitis and carpal tunnel syndrome.

THE COMPUTER AND YOUR LEARNING STYLE

If you learn best by moving, you'll probably find computers especially engaging.

If you learn best by hearing, some computers have microphones you can speak into—some even have a built-in voice component that will read back what you've written. If English is not your first language, this can be quite helpful!

If you are a visual learner, you'll probably find the icons and symbols available on many computer software programs, helpful. The little pictures *show* you what to do!

WRITE AND DOODLE

Have scrap paper handy for doodling in addition to your notebook or tape recorder. Doodling will help loosen up your mind and give you small breaks during intense study periods. It's also a good idea to re-write your notes. Writing them over will help you understand and remember them better. You can re-organize them as you write them, too. Writing, after all, is a physical activity!

There's Action—and There's Action

Kinesthetic learning takes different forms in different people.

- Jake hates sports, but he's active in other ways. His hands move like butterflies when he speaks. He's successful in his marketing career. He likes working with people, and he likes the frequent activity of checking merchandise and prices.
- Katie's friends say she's quiet. She likes listening to music and knitting. She often doodles when she's thinking—on the phone, in class, or on the bus to work. She feels knitting and doodling help her stay calm and think clearly.
- Tara loves playing basketball and ice skating. In class, she's usually tapping her foot. In fact, it's sometimes difficult for her not to tap her foot.

Jake, Katie, and Tara learn best when they're moving in some way. The ways vary, but they are all kinesthetic learners.

Want other suggestions? Use the tips listed in the beginning of this chapter. The section "Becoming an Active Learner" provides fun and effective exercises for developing your kinesthetic study skills.

ANOTHER ACTIVE LEARNING TECHNIQUE

Experienced active learners think ahead before they read, and then think back about what they've just read. Now that you're at the end of the chapter, go back to what you wrote or recorded at the beginning of it.

- How does what happened in this chapter compare with what you expected to happen?
- How would you answer the questions you had at the beginning of the chapter?
- And the biggie: What was most useful to you in this chapter?

In Short

There are different ways of "doing" in learning. One is to become actively involved through making your own questions and finding your own answers—making the material personally interesting to you.

Another way is to actually move about. Walking, for example, can help clear your head and help you remember what you learned. Some people learn best by moving.

Practice Tips

- **Study actively.** Before you study, think of a real-life use for the subject at hand. Imagine yourself as a professional involved with the study material. If you're studying management, pretend you own your own company; if you're studying chemistry, think of yourself as a chemist; and so on. Keep your character in mind as you create and answer questions from the text or audiotape, make notes, and review your study session.
- **Study by moving.** After a study session, take a notepad and pen with you as you go for a walk of at least 20 minutes. Choose a time when you don't feel rushed. As you're walking, think about what you studied. Stop and write down these thoughts as they come to mind. You might also discover new connections with old material.

CHAPTER | 6

MAKING STUDYING DO-ABLE

Break up a major study project into pieces and it won't seem so impossible. Make a plan based on your unique learning style and stick to it. Take into consideration how much time you have before the exam, how difficult the material is for you, and where and when you study best. The key here is to study "brick by brick," making a study project—whether reading a long chapter or writing a major paper—less intimidating and more do-able.

The next time you're in a group, ask each person how long it took them to learn to ride a bike, type, or drive a car. Chances are you'll have a different answer from each person. Someone might have learned in two months, someone else in two years, another person in two weeks—or maybe even two days! Everyone has their own rate of learning. And it *varies*, depending on what it is you're learning. When you're developing a time-management study plan, you need to keep in mind how *you* learn.

TIME MANAGEMENT
USING A CALENDAR

Use your calendar as a study planner. There are endless possibilities of how to do this; find the way that works best for you. Below are a couple of suggestions.

One Color Per Course

Use a different color ink for each course you have to study for. Record what you'd like done when, for each course in its color, all on the same calendar. Your calendar might end up looking like a rainbow, but you'll have a clearer idea of each deadline.

Set Three Deadlines

Write on the calendar the dates:

- You *must* have your project finished
- You'd *like* to have it finished
- You'd like to have it *almost* finished

Using multiple deadlines works especially well if you're the type of person who sets your clock ahead five or ten minutes. It's always wise to get a project finished ahead of time because, like Murphy's Law, if something *can* go wrong, it will. If you often have to put in overtime at your job, or have fluctuating family responsibilities, set your "almost finished" deadline at least two weeks before your final deadline. Staying on top of a project, be it studying for a big exam, writing a paper, or completing a major lab report, will give you the sense of control you need to study effectively.

Divide a Task into Smaller Steps

Big tasks can be broken up into small stages, each with its own deadline. For example, if your assignment is to read a book and then write a report about it, you could set up four stages for the project:

1. Read the book, taking notes as you go;
2. Review your notes and prepare questions for your report
3. Write a draft of your report
4. Edit and polish the report into finished form.

Set a separate deadline for each stage by breaking up the time between now and the report's due date. Allocate less time for the easier stages and more for tougher ones.

If, after you've thought it all through, you see that you would work better if there were even more steps with more interim (in-between) deadlines, add them in. For instance, you might want to divide both your reading and writing the rough draft into two steps each.

DEALING WITH DEADLINES
If You Work Well with Deadlines

Arrange to meet with a friend or study buddy at least every two weeks, or once a week if you can. During your meetings, show and explain to your partner what you've done since you last met. Having someone else keep track of your progress will provide outside pressure, encouraging you to keep up with your deadlines. (Chapter 16, "Working with Your Study Buddy," will go into this in more detail.)

If Deadlines Make You Nervous

Give yourself *plenty* of time! Working steadily and regularly prevents last-minute pressure. You'll find tips on how to do this in Chapter 1, "Getting Started." Do what it takes to keep calm and cool—even if it means reading or writing in the bathtub!

Juggling Several Projects at Once

What if you have more than one study project due at the same time? Think of it as building all the walls of your house, a bit at a time, so the four walls will be finished together. Start the more complicated project, or the more challenging subject immediately. Give it 20 minutes at a time, more or less, depending on your learning tempo. Weave in study time for the other subjects, using one as a study break from the others. Devote smaller amounts of time to simpler projects, but be careful not to neglect them entirely.

MAKING TIME

You want to make the most of the time of day that works best for you, particularly if you're learning something new. But you can also make good use of less optimal times during your day. Remember, every little bit counts. Six study periods of ten minutes each make a total of one full hour. Try any of the following times in your day-to-day schedule to see which of them work for you.

While Showering or Working Out

Perhaps a good time to study is the time you have to yourself while you're in the shower, or running, walking, or doing other exercise. With few other distractions, you can be thinking about what you've recently read or learned in a class. Consider it your physical—and mental—tune-up time.

On Your Way to Work or Class

If you take a bus, train, or ferry, you can listen to tapes on a headset or read and write in your notebook or reading log. (See Chapter 10, "Getting More Out of Reading," for creating and working with reading logs.) If you drive, you can listen to a tape (but not a headset—you might not be able to hear an emergency vehicle), or you can be thinking about something you've read recently.

At Lunch

This can be a good time to read and write in your reading log. If you routinely lunch with others, excuse yourself early or reserve a couple of lunchtimes a week for some studying.

While Doing Chores

Household chores occupy your hands, but free your mind—and ears—for thinking, talking (even if it's to yourself!), and listening to tapes. For example:

- **If you learn best by hearing**: You can listen to a taped lecture, notes you recorded on audiotape, or a book on tape while you wash dishes.
- **If you learn best by doing**: You might want to go back and forth, spending 10 to 20 minutes on reading and/or writing, then 10 to 20 minutes on meal preparation, and so on.

At Bedtime

You are most apt to remember something when you are very relaxed, so bedtime can be ideal study time—so long as you're not dead tired.

Change your routine so that you get to bed about half an hour earlier than usual. Read something you want to remember for 20 minutes or less just before you go to sleep. Or listen to a tape, if you learn best by hearing. Your subconscious will hold onto what you read or heard while you sleep. Read or listen to the same material again right after you wake up. Remember to use the learning styles—reading aloud, drawing pictures—that work best for you.

You can also use this technique if you are trying to come up with an idea or a solution. Pose the question to yourself just before going to sleep. Chances are, you'll wake up with an answer!

THE RIGHT TIME FOR THE RIGHT TASK

Two of the most important phases of studying are absorbing new material and reviewing old. It is important to perform these tasks when you're at your best. Making connections is also essential in the learning process; you can make connections any time of day.

Learning New Material

New material will be absorbed more readily if you study when you're comfortable and your mind is fresh. Try getting up a little earlier than usual in the morning to study while you have fewer distractions.

New material stays in a certain part of your brain—a kind of holding area—for only three days or so. To ensure that you cement it more permanently in your memory, review the material as soon as possible.

Reviewing Old and New Material

Reviewing new material is less challenging than learning it in the first place, but still takes lots of "brain energy." Before and after sleep are good times for review. Make sure you use your learning styles (see Chapters 2 through 5).

Reviewing old material is just as important, especially when you're studying for a final exam that covers topics from the beginning of the year. It's easy to say, "I don't need to review; I've already studied it once." But your brain needs a refresher course. Reviewing old material regularly in small bits is much more effective, and less hectic, than trying to review everything the night before the test.

You can even review without your study material—on a train, in your car sitting in traffic, or waiting at the doctor's office. Just think about what you know already—and why it's important to you. Be ready for any new questions you might ask yourself! Jot them down as soon as you can.

Making Connections

Relating new material to what you already know can be done any time. Ask yourself, "What does this remind me of?" as you go about your daily routine. Carry a small notebook with you to write down thoughts as they come. It's a good idea to have a special notebook for any project you're working on, small enough to carry with you. Ideas can come at *any* time; you can be waiting for a bus or putting a baby to bed. Be ready!

Finding multiple times in your day to study means you can keep going. Your hard work will pay off. However, make sure you also get plenty of rest, eat well, and treat yourself occasionally! A good mood keeps you motivated and energized.

USE YOUR LEARNING STYLE

Before you plunge into a new study project, consider your past successes. Think about a project you did, and what you did to successfully complete it. Which of the following applies to you?

Do you like to stick with one thing at a time? This usually appeals to *literal* (often left-handed) and *sequential* learners. If so, use different days to focus on different subjects. It is a good idea to allot additional short study periods to review new material in other subjects, so every subject is studied nearly every day.

Do you prefer going back and forth between different things? This usually appeals to *kinesthetic* and *image* learners. If so, warn the people who live and work with you that you need space to lay out material! When working on several projects at the same time, it is a good idea to take breaks between each. Kinesthetic and image learners should be prepared for ideas coming at any time—even when working on a project in another subject. Are you more comfortable standing, sitting, or lying down? Maybe you need to vary your position from project to project.

If You Learn Best with Images

Focus on parts of the assignment where pictures come most easily to mind. In your notebook or into your tape recorder, describe the pictures you imagine. As you review the material you're studying, go back to your notebook or tape recorder and add detail. Notice how your picture becomes more complete as you begin to further understand the topic at hand.

Image, or global, learners often are good at seeing the big picture and the connections between things, but perhaps at the sacrifice of the finer details. You can compensate for this by having a family member, friend, or study buddy remind you of your due dates.

If You Learn Best with Order

You might be more comfortable following sequential lessons or sections of what you're reading or listening to. For instance, if you had a deadline to finish this book, you might divide the book into four parts and make a smaller deadline for each quarter. Or perhaps you'd order the chapters in decreasing degrees of difficulty. In that case, you'd study the most difficult material first and the easiest last. Find the order that's best for you.

If You Learn Best by Seeing

Write or draw as you study. If you're using an audiotape, write what you hear. Use colored markers to create our own color code. Give each color a "job." In math, use a different color for each operation, so you *see* where you're multiplying and where you're adding. Do the same in studying a text or writing in your notebook: use a certain color to take notes on details in a certain subject. This lets you *see* how different facts are connected to each other. For instance, in studying history, you might note facts leading to the French Revolution in one color, details of the revolution itself in another, and results of the revolution in a third color, and so on.

If You Learn Best by Hearing

Talk and listen. Read texts aloud, and read your notes out loud into a tape recorder, so you can review by re-listening. Use different intonations as you read, to organize related information. In the example above, you could speak in a low tone for events leading up to the French Revolution, sing notes on events during the revolution, and chant to denote the results of the revolution. As you reflect on what you studied, try to hear your notes in your head. You may want to check your school or local library for relevant tapes; there's a chance the book you're reading is on tape.

GETTING STARTED
BEGIN WITH THE EASIEST

You'll feel good when you've finished *something*. Anything. Choose the task that takes the least amount of time. For example:

- If you have a seven-page lesson to study, begin by just making sense of the title. Write in your notebook or talk into a tape recorder about what it means to you.
- If you are about to solve math or science problems, choose the simplest problem first. Write in your notebook what you did to solve the problem. Draw pictures that help you see the probleml in your head.

KEEP FOCUSED

Before you start your science project or begin to study for that test, decide how long you want each study session to be. Can each be 20 minutes long? That's about how long most people can stay really focused on the task at hand. But perhaps it's less for you—maybe 10 or 15 minutes. Or maybe it's more like 25 or 30 minutes. Whatever you find is best for you, try to stick to it.

Remind yourself that you have a regular period of time to stay focused, but don't be so rigid that it can't change sometimes for legitimate reasons, such as when:

- You're familiar with the material and can move ahead easily without difficulty.
- You're ill.
- You really enjoy the material and want to stay with it longer.

IN SHORT

You'll remember more if you break your study project into smaller chunks instead of trying to tackle it all at once. Use a calendar to plan ahead, setting several short and reasonable deadlines for yourself. Get a general idea of what you'll be studying, then build on what you already know. Use those study techniques that have worked best for you in the past.

Practice Tip

Take a short break after reading this chapter, then spend 20 minutes (more or less!) *today* on beginning your study project. Make sure you reward yourself when you stick to your schedule!

CHAPTER | 7

What makes you say, "Now I get it!" or "I see what you mean"? You have learned something—whether it's parallel parking a car or understanding terms in a psychology class—when you know that you know it.

KNOWING WHAT YOU KNOW

Knowing something and *knowing that* you know something are two different things. You may know things you don't *know* you know—odd little facts lying around in your head like Ted Williams' batting average or the phone number of your childhood home. On the other hand, you can *think* you know something that you don't *really* know, like the contents of that chapter you read or lecture you heard but didn't think about afterwards. To study effectively, you have to realize what you don't really know. It is then that you will develop an *awareness* of your knowledge and learning processes.

It is not easy to develop awareness. You must bring up to the level of consciousness things you've more or less taken for granted, things you've let lie low. Awareness is like a cog in the machinery of the brain, because it helps you move and connect other information. Another word for awareness is *cognition*. Cognition is knowing when you know something.

What Is Awareness?

Shirley read the assigned lesson on thinking for her psychology class. She felt she knew the material she studied. Yet, in class when the instructor started talking about cognition, she felt lost. She looked at Charlene sitting next to her, and whispered, "I don't remember reading about that!" "It's here, on page 27," Charlene answered, showing Shirley the textbook. Shirley asked Charlene after class, "How could I think I understood something, when I didn't?"

Charlene laughed, "That's just what the lesson was about— needing awareness so you know when you know, and know when you don't." Shirley shook her head, "I felt really involved reading about the experiments with the monkey in the beginning of the lesson. I guess I just skimmed over the rest of the reading, so I thought the whole lesson was on the monkey. It's obvious that I didn't read it carefully enough."

BUILDING AWARENESS

Realizing exactly how you go about mentally processing what you read and hear may not come naturally to you. It's difficult because reading and hearing are things people do automatically. For example, someone wouldn't say to himself, before opening a book, "I'll open this book now and turn to the page where I left off last time. Then I'll move my eyes across and down each page until I get to the end of this lesson. . . ." He just does it.

How do *you* know when you know something? How do you know for sure? How do you know, for example, that one plus one equals two? You might say, "Of course, I know it!" But—*how* do you know you know it?

Use your own learning styles to build an awareness of what you know:

- **If you learn best by seeing**: You might say, "Here's one pencil, and here's another pencil. I can see there are two pencils."

- **If you learn best by hearing**: You might say, "Here's the sound of one pencil making a tap on the table, and here's the sound of a second pencil tap. I hear two taps."

- **If you learn best by images**: You might say, "I know one plus one makes two because I picture one pencil and then the other and I see that there are two."

- **If you learn best by ordering things**: You might say, "The order is right. I know that I start with two individual pencils and end up with a pair."

- **If you learn best by doing**: You might pick up one pencil and pick up another, and say, "I see them, I feel them. Here they are, one plus one equals two."

There can be many different ways to know that you know; you just have to figure out which way is yours.

PUTTING AWARENESS TO THE TEST

It's one thing to *think* you know, and another to actually know. Test yourself to find out how well you know something you are studying.

SEEING IS BELIEVING

One way you know something is by seeing it in your head. Using images to reconstruct what you brought away from chemistry class, a good movie, or a dance recital comes naturally for many people. Charlene, who we met in the beginning of this chapter, knows she learns well using images. Read on to see how she made sense of the cognition chapter.

Charlene checked to see that she knew what she thought she knew by drawing a picture of her study material. Since the images that came to her mind were so clear she could draw a detailed and coherent picture, she was able to say, "I know that I know this because the pictures are clear in my head."

MAKING ORDER

Another way to test your understanding of what you've studied is to review the order of events. Charlene also used an order-oriented approach to supplement her picture:

Charlene listed events and drew a timeline to demonstrate what she absorbed from studying. This helped her notice where the part about the monkey ended and the definition of cognition began. She was able to say, "I know that the subject is changing because there is a clear sequence of events."

THE QUEST FOR QUESTIONS

Another way to check yourself is to come up with questions. Charlene was an extremely thorough student, and ended up answering all her own questions.

Charlene came up with several questions based on her picture and timeline. She then went back to her text and answered those questions and changed her picture and timeline until they were both clear. Then, when she had no more questions, she was sure she knew the material. At that point, the picture and the timeline were clear in her mind, the order of events was clear, and the timeline and picture were obviously related. Then she was able to say, "I get it!"

BUILDING ON WHAT YOU ALREADY KNOW

Thinking about what you've read or listened to helps you identify what you know, and this helps you make sense of what you studied. When you can connect new material to things you already know, you learn the material faster and remember it longer.

The best way to make connections between new and old material is to use your learning styles. Use the ideas below to build on what you already know. The more connections you make between and within topics, the more coherent your study material will become.

- **If you learn best by seeing:** Compare old notes to new notes; look for common words and phrases, and make connections between ideas.

- **If you learn best by hearing:** Read your notes aloud. Listen for familiar words and phrases. Where have you heard them before?

- **If you learn best by making images:** Draw pictures or maps of what you see when you study. Do these images bring to mind something you've learned in the past?

- **If you learn best by order:** First review old material and then take a look at a new assignment in the same subject. Make a timeline or list of events starting from the old material and working through the new. See how things progressed, or didn't.

- **If you learn best by doing:** Role play. If you're reading a novel, act out the part of the hero or heroine. Does that character remind you of anyone you know? This familiarity could help you write your essay.

As you try one or more of these methods, are you *aware* of how you are studying? Think, write, or talk about it.

DISCOVERING THE FAMILIAR

Here's a sample version of how you can use what's familiar to help you learn and remember something that's unfamiliar.

- Skim through a page of a text you're studying or a newspaper and find a word that's new to you—for example, the word *crumpet.*
- Find parts of that word you already know: *crum* and *pet* or *et.*
- In your notebook, write down other words that have the same letters as those in the parts you've identified: *crumb* and *petty.*
- What similar meaning is in your list of words? You might say that *crumb* is a small piece of food and *petty* describes something that doesn't matter very much.

Now you have a general idea of what the new word could mean. For example, *crumpet* could mean a small piece of food that's not important. To be sure, you may want to check your definition with the dictionary's definition. For example, the dictionary definition of *crumpet* is "a light bread, often toasted." By coming to *your* definition first, you've made what you learned meaningful to you. And you've used *cognition*. You used what you already knew!

IN SHORT

The first step in studying is to recognize what you know. You *know* when you know something when:

- You can make clear images in your mind of what you're studying.
- What you're reading or listening to follows a clear order.
- You've answered all your own questions.

Practice Tips

The next time you study, test if you really know a paragraph:

- Draw a picture or a cartoon of what the paragraph was about. Then, write a paragraph describing your picture or cartoon. How are they similar? The more similar your paragraph is to the paragraph you're studying, the more you *know* the paragraph.
- Make a timeline, showing the order of events in the paragraph. Check by going back to the paragraph.
- Draw lines connecting the pictures to the events listed on the timeline.

CHAPTER | 8

You can only find an
answer when you have a
question. Once you've
identified what you
already know in your
study material, you can
find out what you don't
know. Then you can
create questions, and
then look for the
answers. And then,
you'll have learned
something!

KNOWING WHEN YOU DON'T KNOW

How often have you heard someone say, "I don't know"? That phrase is the key to studying. What separates experienced students from inexperienced ones is awareness of what they know and what they don't know. Those with academic experience know enough to ask the specific questions that will help them find the answers. Once they've found those answers, they've learned something new.

Separating Known From Unknown

George was studying geometry. "I know the answer!" he exclaimed when Abe asked him to work on a problem with him. "How do you know it?" Abe asked. "Well, I know what an equilateral triangle is because I see the word *equal* in it. That clues me to the fact that an equilateral triangle is a triangle with three equal sides."

"I know that, too," Abe said, "but I still don't know how to find the area of the equilateral triangle."

"Oh, you're right; I don't either," George said, looking at the problem again. "I jumped ahead too quickly; I only recognized what I knew about the problem, not what I didn't know. Let's look at this together. Maybe we can find something else we know that will help solve the problem."

FINDING OUT WHAT YOU DON'T KNOW

After each study session, and after each class or lecture you attend, your final step must be to reflect on what you learned in that session or class. Thinking about the session lets you check what you know for sure and what you don't know.

The writer of your textbook, or the lecturer in your class, is taking you on a trip to some place you've never been before, and that "place" is a new piece of knowledge or a new set of facts. When the trip is over—when you've read the chapter or heard the lecture—you need to ask yourself the following questions:

- Where was the writer or teacher trying to take me? That is, what was the main idea of this reading or lecture?
- How did I get there? What were the steps that led to this main idea?
- Have I arrived? Do I understand this main idea and all the steps that led up to it?

Chapter 7, "Knowing What You Know" showed you how to know when you know for sure. You *know* that you know the material when you have:

- A clear picture in your mind
- A clear sense of order
- No remaining questions in your mind

The problem is that sometimes you can think you know more than you do. That is why it's important to actually *draw* your picture and *write* down the order. When you come to the point that you can't proceed with your drawing or list, you've hit the point where you should start asking questions.

Another way to find out what you know and what you don't is to role play. Pretend you are the writer of your textbook, or your teacher. If you have a study buddy (see Chapter 16, "Working with a Study Buddy"), one of you can be the writer or teacher and the other the student. Explain to your study buddy what you just read or heard. If you don't have a study buddy, explain it to yourself. Make sure you don't leave out any steps!

When you come to any point where your explanation is unclear, when it might not make sense to another person, you've found out what you don't know. That's when it's time to start asking questions. Once you have questions, you can find the answers, and then you will know something that you didn't know before.

THE QUEST IS ON!

Finding what you know and then finding what you don't know is something you already know how to do. If you were in an unfamiliar town and wanted to get to Adams Street, you would know that you don't know how to get there, and you would ask directions.

Those directions would be based on what you already know—your location at the time. You're in the park, and you've been told Adams Street is near the park, but you don't know which direction to go. So you ask. And someone tells you to walk north till you get to the end of the park and then turn left and walk one block to Adams Street.

You might have one more question: Which way is north? And if you get an answer, you'd follow those directions, walking to the end of the park and turning left. So then you get to a street, but it doesn't have a street sign. How do you know if you've arrived? You stop someone passing by and ask again.

ASKING QUESTIONS, GETTING ANSWERS

The process of asking questions to find out, first, what you already know, and second, what you still need to learn, is similar. You might have to ask more than one question as you find your way to the knowledge the writer is trying to give you. Here's a sequence you can go through to find out what you don't know and then ask questions and get answers. If you have been reading a book, the text you'll go back to for answers is the book; if you listened to a lecture, your "text" is your notes or audiotape of the lecture.

1. Draw a picture and write down the order.

2. Is this perfectly clear? Where are the gaps?

3. Ask yourself a question that will help fill in the gap.

4. Go back to your text to find the answer. Use the parts of your picture or outline that are clear to help you see where in the text you should look for the answer. Look in the sections of your text that come right after the last clear piece of your picture or outline.

5. Read the relevant part of the text. Don't try to re-read the whole chapter or go over the whole lecture; you're just looking for one little piece of information, the answer to your question. Take it in small chunks.

6. If you don't have an answer, re-read the same section to try again.

7. If you still don't have an answer, read the parts that come just before and just after what you were reading. Repeat this process until you find the answer to your question.

8. Put this new piece of information into your picture and order. Is the picture clear now? Is the order clear?

9. Keep going back and forth between your study aids and the text until your picture and order are perfectly clear, and you have no questions left.

Now you've really learned something! You have a clear picture of the main idea, and you know all the steps it takes to get there. But notice that this clear picture and order don't come out all at once. You have to take it one step at a time, just as if you were following the directions to Adams Street. And you're always using what you know to help you find the answers to what you don't know.

Here's an example of how you use what you know to help you create questions: Suppose you had to fill in the blank in the following sentence:

When you don't know something, your brain rushes to _____e it has stored ideas on a similar topic.

In order to figure out what word should go in the blank, you should go through the following process:

First ask yourself, "What do I know for sure about the sentence? " Your responses might be:

- I know that the sentence is about recognizing when I don't know something.
- I know that it's about the brain moving in some way.
- I know that there's a storing place in my brain.
- I know that the missing word connects the brain moving to the storage place.
- I know that the missing word ends with *e*.

Then ask yourself, "What kind of word would connect the brain rushing and the storage place?" The word must have something to do with direction. You make up more questions by connecting the words you know that have to do with direction to the sentence:

- Is the word *over*? *Over* doesn't end with the letter *e*.
- Is it *here*? That's a direction word that ends in *e*, but *here* doesn't make sense in this sentence. Filling in that word doesn't give you a clear picture and a clear sense of order.
- You reject *there* for the same reason. The only word that really works in the sentence—that gives a clear picture and order—is *where*.

This was a simple example, but it shows you how to use what you already know to arrive at the answers to the questions about what you don't know.

Choose one paragraph from a book you are studying now. Write down the following in your notebook, or record it onto your audiotape:

- Identify what you know for sure by drawing a picture and writing down the order.
- Find what you don't know.
- Ask questions.
- Go through the steps listed above to find the answers.
- Write or record additional questions as they come to mind.

IT'S ALL YOURS

The questions that count most are *your* questions. You get more out of studying; you become more involved, enjoy it more, it "sticks" more, when you make:

- Your own observations of what you know
- Your own connections of new material to old
- Your own questions and then find your own answers!

Often, the search for answers leads to more questions. And the more questions you ask, the clearer you're making your answers.

YOU'RE IN COMMAND!

You're taking control of your own learning when you:

- Recognize what you know
- Recognize what you don't know
- Create questions to make the pictures in your head and the order of events clear
- Discover answers to your questions
- Realize when and how to question what you've studied

HOW TO ASK QUESTIONS, DEPENDING ON YOUR LEARNING STYLE

The most effective ways to ask questions are different for people with different learning styles.

- **If you learn best by seeing:** Write or draw what you know, and what questions you have.

- **If you learn best by hearing:** Read aloud as you write, and/or use a tape recorder.

- **If you learn best by images:** Draw or describe the pictures and/or maps in your head. Focus on when the pictures are *unclear*. Ask questions to clear your pictures.

- **If you learn best by order:** Make a list and/or timeline—focus on when that's unclear; ask questions to develop a clearer order.

- **If you learn best by doing:** Imagine yourself experiencing what you're studying. Focus on when the experience feels unclear; ask questions to make the experience clearer, more real.

IN SHORT

You need to know what you *do* know in order to find what you *don't* know. Reflect on what you've studied. Thinking about what you've read or listened to lets you find what you know for sure, and what you don't. Ask yourself questions so the picture in your head is clear, and the events are in an order that makes sense to you.

Practice Tips

In the text you're studying, or in a newspaper, find a word you don't know. Cover that word. Look at the rest of the sentence and decide what the sentence could mean without the word you covered. If the sentence isn't clear on its own, write what you know for sure about the meaning of the sentence. Try to draw a picture of the sentence, or to make sense of it in any way that suits your learning style. Now, ask yourself what you need to know to make the sentence clearer. Write down your questions or record them into an audiotape.

Then go back to the original sentence and choose a word or phrase that could replace the unfamiliar word. Check to see that your word or phrase makes your picture clearer. You made a definition based on what you knew—the words around the unknown word—to find out what you didn't know.

Now look in the dictionary and see how close you came!

CHAPTER | 9

You pay closer attention to what you're learning, and even enjoy the process, when what you're studying interests you. Even if something doesn't naturally interest you, you can make it interesting by connecting it with something you already know. When you can build on what you already know, you're more likely to remember what you learned.

GETTING INVOLVED IN LEARNING

Have you had the experience of sitting in a waiting room and picking up a magazine simply for something to do? Maybe it's a magazine on a hobby you're not at all interested in. But, it looks like you'll have a long wait, so you begin looking through it. You begin feeling bored. Then something catches your eye. Maybe it's a photograph of a place you'd like to visit. Maybe it's an article on including pets in a hobby. You become interested. You find yourself getting into the magazine so much that you're almost disappointed when it's time for your appointment

You become interested in something new—something you haven't learned before—when you can relate it to something you already know.

USE YOUR HIDDEN CAMERA

Have you ever looked at the front page of a newspaper and suddenly seen something familiar pop out at you? Maybe someone with the same first name as you was being quoted. Or your hometown was mentioned. You didn't really read the article; the name or the name of the town just seemed to flash before you. Or, maybe you were walking past a clothing store, and out of the corner of your eye you saw "your" slacks on display. They weren't really your slacks, but they were very much like the ones you have. They were so familiar to you that you noticed them without looking for them.

What's at work here is your "hidden camera." When you look at something quickly, such as when you skim a newspaper article, that camera can zoom in on a word, name, or phrase it recognizes. When you use your hidden camera, you're taking the first step to becoming interested.

You can become interested in what you're about to study in the same way you became interested in the waiting-room magazine. Use your hidden camera to find something you already know. Skim what you're about to read—you're not reading for meaning here, only to become interested! You're just looking for something you've seen before. Once you've found it, read around that part first. Enjoy yourself. Then read around other familiar parts. You're likely to find that what you have to read no longer seems strange—you're interested! Then you're ready to begin the real reading.

THE EAR HAS A HIDDEN CAMERA, TOO!

Just as you can see without looking, you can hear without listening. Have you ever been near enough to a group of people to hear that they're talking, but not close enough to be able to hear what they're saying? Or maybe you weren't paying attention because your attention was on something else. Then one person said something really familiar, perhaps your name or your hometown. You automatically stopped whatever else you were thinking or doing and tuned into their conversation. You didn't mean to overhear what they were saying, but that familiar thing just seemed to pop out at you. Because you heard it, you might've tried to hear what else was being said. That's when you became *interested*.

Try using your ear's hidden camera the next time you're listening to an audiotape—whether it's a speech you're studying or a recording of notes you made. Skim the tape. Listen for what's especially familiar. Write down what interests you. Then you're ready to listen to the whole tape. You'll be paying more attention because you've found something that interests you.

GETTING FAMILIAR

Often, the more we know about something (or someone!), the more interested we are.

FAMILIARITY BREEDS INTEREST

Think of someone you like, but who took some time to get to know. Write in your notebook your response to this question:

What is the difference between the way I first felt about Lauren, and the way I feel about her now?

You probably feel closer to Lauren now because at one time you noticed something you both had in common, something you could *relate* to. That motivated you to find out more about her. "Oh, you like movies, too?" you may have asked. When Lauren said "Yes," you wanted to find out more, so perhaps you asked, "What kind of movies do you prefer? Who are your favorite actors?"

Getting to know a subject or text can be a lot like getting to know a friend. The more interests you find, the more comfortable you'll feel with what you're studying, and the more you'll learn.

IT'S ALL RELATIVE

Relatives have something in common. Tony has Uncle Jake's nose. Beryl has her grand-aunt's eyes. What is new (Tony and Beryl) is related to what is known (Uncle Jake and the grand-aunt). There is a connection between the relatives (nose and eyes). When you add new information to what you already know, you make a shared connection. To learn, you need to relate what's new to what you already know.

RELATING TO SOMETHING NEW

Look at whatever is around you, no matter where you are as you read this. Choose two items that you see that are different from each other. For example, you might pair a pencil with a stapler, and a speed bump with a tree. Write in your notebook two things that the items have in common. If you don't know how to start, think about what you know about each item, then ask yourself some questions: "What could a pencil and a stapler have in common?" or "How could a speed bump have anything to do with a tree?" When you find even one answer, you've *related* one item to the other!

Note First, Then Question

You might have answered your question with something you noticed: "Well, the pencil and stapler are both used in office work," or "The speed bump is on the ground, and the tree grows from the ground." Then, you asked another question, such as: "What else do they have in common?" You studied them some more, and noticed something like, "The inside of the pencil is the same color as the stapler," or "The top of the tree is rounded, and so is the top of the speed bump."

You've just done a scientific analysis! You noted your observations and made connections. You do this, too, in reading or listening. You make note of what you recognize, ask yourself how that can relate to something else, and discover your answers and connections as you study.

The way you answer your questions shows *your* interests. If your interests aren't the same as mine (and the chance that we are exactly alike is very small), your answers will probably be different from mine! Different people have different interests—and different ways of relating what they've learned to what they know.

USE YOUR INTERESTS!

You can become more involved with studying if you start with what you like.

If You Are Reading

Skim the text to find something you're interested in. Start backwards, if you'd like. If it's a book, check the table of contents or index. Choose a topic you like, and begin reading there. As you read, remember to take notes or make drawings in your notebook, or speak into your tape recorder. Record what was important or useful to you, as well as what was confusing. Copy the sentence or phrase you'd like to remember, noting the page it's on.

If You Are Listening

If it's an audiotape, listen to it once, just to get started. Then write in your notebook what interested you most about what you heard. Return to that part of the tape and listen to it again.

If you're listening to a lecture or speech, you don't have the opportunity to hear the whole thing once before you start. In that case, you have to try to get interested before the talk begins. Does the lecture have a title, for instance? Perhaps something in that title, if you think about it, will remind you of something you know. Are there any audio-visual aids in the room? Have you been given a handout? Any of these things can help you find out what's interesting to you about the talk before it begins. If the speaker hasn't given you any aids, focus on the speaker him- or herself. Does this look like a person you would trust to give you good information or advice? Does he or she look like someone you know? Even focusing on the speaker's appearance may help you become interested in what the speaker has to say.

ACTING OUT

What if you're studying something and, despite your best efforts, you don't find anything of particular interest in it? Sometimes you just can't find anything that you can connect with.

In that case, pretend you're someone else who *can* relate to the material and has an interest in it! You can *become* interested in a subject when you involve yourself in it, even when you're just role-playing. (See Chapter 5, "Learning by Doing," for more on role-playing and other ways to be an active learner.)

- Pretend you're the instructor; decide what will be the focus of the next class. Let that direct your studying.

- Act! Take on somebody else's interests. If you're studying management, for example, assume the role of a business executive. If you're studying for a science course, pretend you're a research biologist. And so on.

You'll find yourself more responsible for your own learning when you use your interests to connect with what you're studying. The material will be more meaningful to you and you'll enjoy it more. Then you'll remember it better!

IN SHORT

Use what interests you. Find something familiar in what you're studying and build on it to help make sense of newer material. You can also become interested in something by taking on someone else's interests. You can pretend you're the instructor, or you can act the part of someone connected to the subject you're studying. When you use interest as your foundation in study, you're assuming more responsibility for your studying. You're making it meaningful to *you*.

Practice Tips

The next time you're looking at a newspaper, choose a section you rarely read. Choose any article in that section.

- Start with the headline. Make it interesting to you by finding a familiar word or phrase and thinking about what you already know about it.
- Use your hidden camera and skim the article to find something else familiar.
- Assume the part of someone in the article who is being quoted. Move around and act as you imagine that person might act as you read the quote aloud.
- What else do you need to know to understand the article? Write a list of questions you have. Direct some of the questions to the reporter who wrote the article, and some of the questions to someone quoted in the article.
- Now you're ready to read the article—with interest!

CHAPTER | 10

You can make more sense of what you're reading when you get involved with it. And you can do this by anticipating what you read before you begin. While you read, ask questions, make pictures in your head, take notes, and use your learning styles. Stop when you don't know something, wait until you understand it, and then continue with the reading. After you've finished reading, think about what you've learned.

GETTING MORE OUT OF READING

Here's a hard but not surprising truth: *Reading is work.* It can be easy and enjoyable work, like reading a good story or the comics. Or, it can be more challenging work, such as reading a textbook or other study material.

Now think a minute about work. If you show up at your job and just sit there till quitting time, did you work? No, you put in your time, but you didn't work—and if you keep acting that way, you'll get fired. It's the same way with reading. If you just sit there, moving your eyes over the page, you aren't really reading—and you're not getting anything out of it. To get the most out of what you read, you have to get actively involved in the material. Your mind should be working before, while, and after you read.

There's Reading—and There's Reading

"I just don't get this marine biology book. I can't understand the first chapter. I read it, and I don't get anything out of it," Sally complains to Harry.

"How are you reading it?" Harry asks.

"What do you mean—how?" she answers.

"Well, how involved are you with what you're reading?"

"What do you mean—involved? Reading is like TV, you look at it and you get meaning," Sally says.

"It sounds like you need to read more actively," Harry tells her. "Reading is very different from watching TV."

Sally has a problem. She expects reading to come to her, like her favorite sitcom on TV. She's not treating reading as work, but rather as a relaxing pastime. Having a difficult reading assignment make sense means asking questions, making connections, and creating order—getting involved!

BEFORE YOU READ

WHAT'S IN A TITLE?

You have a title, even if you didn't win a world heavyweight boxing match. *Mr., Ms., Mrs.,* and *Miss* are titles. In a sense, so are *Mom, Dad, Sis,* and *Brother.* And there are many more. Get out your notebook and list your own titles. Start with your name, your family relationships, and what people call you in a formal setting (like Mr. or Ms.). List your job titles, and any positions you hold in volunteer or professional organizations.

Like people, chapters, lessons, and books have titles that tell you what they're about. Just as you know Ms. Smith isn't a man, you know the article "Cooking Peas" isn't about carrots. Titles are there to eliminate confusion and give a general impression before the finer details are known. Titles can tell you a lot—don't overlook them!

Test the definition of *title* by applying it to the chapter you are reading now. The chapter title is "Getting More Out of Reading." Read the summary that appears next to the title. It says the same thing as the chapter title, but in more words. The chapter section you're reading now is called "What's in a Title?" It's part of a larger section called "Before You Read." As you make sense of what the author is saying about titles, you're answering the question of this section's title, "What's in a Title?"

GET READY TO READ

Start thinking about what you will be reading before you even begin to read. First, choose a section to read. If the reading is divided into chapters, a chapter is a good place to start. If it's a long chapter with sub-headings, begin with the first sub-heading. Look at the *title* of the chapter, the sub-heading, or the article only. Write down your answers to these questions:

- What does the title make you think of?
- What do you expect the reading to be about?
- What questions do you expect the reading to answer?

If Sally, who we met in the beginning of this chapter, followed this advice, her mind wouldn't start to drift to other things, like what she's doing tonight, or how she's going to get home. She would be actively engaged in deciphering titles in her marine biology book. Making a study plan and sticking to it would help Sally stop daydreaming.

USING ILLUSTRATIONS

If the reading has any illustrations, photographs, or drawings, look at those, too. Write:

- What the illustrations seem to be about
- How the illustrations might connect with the title

When you study the title and illustrations before you read, you are *pre-reading.* You are preparing to read by first getting in touch with what you already know about the topic.

Using Your Own Special Filing System

Your brain has a wonderful filing system. It files everything you have seen, heard, tasted, and felt. All your experiences are up there—both your actual experiences and what you learned through reading, seeing, and listening. Information is stored in different compartments of your brain; each compartment has a specialty.

When you pre-read, you are reminding yourself of information you already know. You're putting yourself right in front of the "file cabinet" you need, ready to pull other information you already know—and ready to add new information. When you pre-read, you are more likely to remember what you've read. You're also more likely to enjoy it because you've begun to connect it with what you already know.

Sally, the marine biology student, remembers her summer trips to the beach as a child. She remembers the different kinds of shells she collected. Her mental file cabinet is ready for new files on marine biology. She begins making sense of what she is reading—and to enjoy and learn from the marine biology book.

AS YOU READ

Now that you've already gotten into the file cabinet in your head by pre-reading, you want to be ready to add new folders or information to your file cabinet. You need to be able to hold onto the new information you'll acquire as you begin to read the article or chapter.

Keeping a Reading Log

When you wrote down or recorded your pre-reading ideas and questions, you began your *reading log*. This is a notebook (or audiotape) that helps you keep track of what you're reading, what it means to you, what questions you have, and what answers you are discovering.

You add to it when you write and/or draw pictures to make sense of new information. It's a good idea to take notes on everything you read. You might want to use thin notebooks that you can easily carry anywhere you find yourself reading. Perhaps your instructor has test booklets you could use for reading logs. These can be folded into a pocket or purse, making it easy to read and take notes while you're just about anywhere— on the bus, on your lunch hour, in the waiting room.

You might want to make a narrow column on each page of your reading log to jot down the page numbers of the text you're writing notes about. This makes it easy for you to go back to check information. If you're expected to write a report on what you read, your log provides you with a head start. In it, you've already written pages that refer to specific information, quotes of what's important or questionable, your feelings on what you read, questions that you had, and what associations and experiences came to mind.

You can also keep a reading log on audiotape, though this is a little less convenient. However, if you're strongly oriented to using your ears rather than your eyes, you may find that speaking into a tape and listening to it later is more useful than writing in a notebook. In that case, make sure you have a small tape recorder you can carry with you anywhere.

This reading log is just for you. No one else will ever see or hear it unless you choose to show it to someone. So you can write or say whatever you want. Even if the associations you make seem a little silly to you, even if your questions seem too stupid to ask in class—write them down. Those silly associations may help you remember, and those stupid questions can't be answered until you ask them, even of yourself.

EXPERIENCE COUNTS!

Every time you read something new, you're adding to your experience. To help you hold onto the new information, continue to connect it with what you already know. If something is new to you and you have little experience that relates to it, be prepared to stop. Stopping helps you remember and gives your brain time to process what you've just learned.

After you've read the first couple of sentences of a reading, ask yourself what it means and how it goes along with your pre-reading idea of what it was going to be about. Look for the main idea of the reading, which is usually found either in an introduction or first paragraph. (You may wish to review Chapter 8, "Knowing When You Don't Know.")

For example, Sally, who is studying marine biology, should stop and ask herself, "What was in that first paragraph that sticks out in my mind? Is this what I expected from reading the title and subheadings of this chapter?" If nothing stands out about the first paragraph or two, she should go back and read them again.

WHEN EXPERIENCE FAILS YOU

What about when there's little of your own experience to connect with the reading? You'll probably have trouble understanding. So stop. Take some time to go over the section that's giving you trouble. Use your reading log, re-read the text, and use your learning style to help you understand.

Put It in Your Reading Log

If you're having trouble understanding something you're reading, start by writing about it or talking into your tape recorder. Ask yourself the following questions:

- What does this make me think of?
- What pictures come to mind?
- What is the most important word in the sentence?

Sally found the book's reference to a marine biology lab strange because she had never been in such a lab. She tried to pretend she was a marine biologist. She used her experience of being in her dentist's office. She thought of the different tools her dentist used, and she applied that to imagining what a marine biologist's office might be like. She decided it would be on a boat. Then she went back to the reading and focused on the word *laboratory*. She felt much more comfortable and secure now that she had formed a picture in her mind. She *knew* what she was reading.

If the text is yours to keep, circle important words, and draw a picture in the margin of what comes to mind. For now, skip over any words you don't know. This way, you'll keep your pace and hold onto the *idea* of what you're reading. If the text is not yours, use scrap paper or, better yet, your reading log.

Re-Read the Text

When a text has you stumped, what do you do? Read the text over again, looking for:

- Images that are clear to you
- An order of events that is clear to you

Once you know which parts you understand, you have a key to help you with the parts you don't understand. Ask yourself, "What do I need to know to make the pictures and order clear?" Perhaps some answers will be found in a passage that comes before the section you're reading. Start with the part you do understand, and use information from the difficult section to add to your picture or order.

If more questions come to mind, read the text over again until you've discovered your answers. You're putting new material into the file cabinet in your head. Don't rush; it takes time. (You may wish to review Chapter 4, "Making Images, Making Order, Making Sense.")

Use Your Learning Style

Use your learning style or styles as you stop and become comfortable with the new material, thinking about what you just read or listened to. Your brain needs time to file what you're learning so you can pull out the file later when you need it for a test. Read aloud, draw pictures or cartoons, make a timeline—whatever works for you. (You might also want to review Chapters 2 through 5 about the different learning styles.)

Go to a chapter you haven't seen yet in this book. Choose a paragraph toward the end of the chapter. Make sure you don't read what comes before the paragraph! Follow the suggestions above for pre-reading and beginning to read. Then read the paragraph, and write your observations and questions in your notebook.

AFTER YOU'VE READ

Most everyone can remember what came first and what came last better than they remember what was in the middle—be it a shopping list or scenes in a play. That's why writers and teachers generally put the nitty-gritty, the main idea, of what you're reading in the beginning, and repeat it at the end.

Every time you complete an assignment, think about what you got out of it. In your reading log, answer these questions:

- What was most useful or interesting about what you read?
- How did the beginning compare with the end?

- What did you disagree with or find confusing?
- What ways of reading worked best for you (reading aloud, drawing pictures, etc.)?

To make sure you have understood what you've read, follow the steps listed in Chapters 7 and 8 on knowing what you know and don't know. Make a picture, make order—and then record any questions you still have left so you can tackle them in your next study session.

NOW YOU SEE IT, NOW YOU DON'T

Here's a secret to reading: Some words have two different kinds of meanings, literal and figurative. One meaning you can feel, see, hear, smell, or taste. It's really there. A second meaning you have to figure out, based on the first meaning.

For instance, think about the word *road*. Imagine the road near you. You can see it; when someone walks or drives on it, you can hear traffic on it; if it's a tar road and a warm day, you can even smell it. A word meaning something that's really there is called *literal*. (You may want to review abstract and literal thinking in Chapter 2, Discovering How You Learn.) If you're a literal (right-brain) learner, literal understanding generally comes readily to you.

Some words also have a symbolic or *abstract* meaning. With the example of *road*, what does a road *do*? It takes you somewhere, right? Now you see that you can use *road* in a different way, an abstract way, a way that does not have a picture—a way that is not literal. Because you have to figure out this kind of meaning, it is called *figurative*. Reading this book might be part of your "road to success." You're getting somewhere—you just can't literally see it. If you're an abstract (left-brain) thinker, this kind of thinking generally comes readily to you.

To get from a *literal* understanding of a word to its *figurative* meaning, try this:

- First, picture the literal meaning in your head.
- Next, write (or tape-record) a description of what the word does.
- Then, hold on to the *idea* of what the word does, and consider its figurative meanings.

Try this approach in going from a literal to figurative understanding with other words. Think about the word *chair*. What does a chair do? It supports you. Were you ever chair of a committee? Get the idea?

Try this with titles, too. What is the literal meaning of a title? What could a figurative meaning be? Notice the title of a film, short story, poem, or play. Often there are two meanings to fiction, one literal—one you can easily picture—and another figurative—one you need to figure out. For example, the film "The Freshman" is about a young man who is in his first year of college (literal) and who is also naive, inexperienced, and "fresh" to the ways of the world (figurative).

If English isn't your first language, be on the look-out for many words and phrases with figurative meanings. To say, "A bell went off in her head," doesn't mean she had an operation, a bell was placed inside her head, and it rang! Instead, ask yourself, What picture comes to mind? A bell ringing. What does a ringing bell signify? It might announce something or call attention to something, right? It brings something to mind that wasn't thought of before. "A bell went off inside her head" figuratively means "She realized something." You'll find that the more practice you have, the easier it will be to go from literal to figurative understanding—from "seeing" something to realizing its figurative, richer meaning!

IN SHORT

To make sense of what you read, first study the title and any illustrations to come up with the main idea of the reading. Come up with questions that the text should answer. You want to have clear images in your head, and a clear sense of the order of events of what you're reading or listening to. Stop when you come to something new or confusing. Connect it with what you already know, to help your brain file it as something learned. After you read, you think back on what you read, and how you read it.

Practice Tips

Practice pre-reading the next time you're reading a newspaper or magazine article, or even watching a film. Pre-read the title of the film or reading matter, and then pay very close attention to what's happening in the beginning. Try to predict the ending, based on what's happening or being discussed at the start. Have fun!

CHAPTER | 11

You're studying a lecture you listened to, or something you've read. You understand it—and now you want to get it to stick! How do you make sure you won't forget it by tomorrow? The trick is to start by identifying what's important to you and relate it to something you know. Then use it in your conversations, write it down, or draw or record it. You get actively involved with the new material, using your learning style.

REMEMBERING WHAT YOU'VE LEARNED

There's a difference between memorizing something and remembering it. Straight memorization doesn't usually stay with you very long. Real learning, on the other hand, lets you apply what you learned. Because you use it, it has meaning for you. Because it has meaning for you, you're apt to remember it!

WHAT'S IMPORTANT TO YOU?

You have your lecture tape and/or notes, you have your reading log and/or tape—you understand what you've read, the lecture made sense to you. You know it now and you want to know it tomorrow and the next day and . . .

Ask yourself, and answer in your notebook:

- What do I want to remember?
- Why is this important to me?

Memorizing vs. Remembering

In his Spanish class, Jeff was given a list of vocabulary words to learn. There were Spanish words in one column and their corresponding English words in the other. Jeff took the list and memorized all the Spanish words. He read them out loud. He put the list on his bedroom mirror, on his refrigerator, in his notebook, and on his TV set. Jeff felt he knew those words. Then came the test. He took one look at it and froze. His Spanish teacher had changed the order of the words, and Jeff had memorized the list in a certain order. He could repeat the exact list, but he couldn't translate them at random. He hadn't learned the words.

Jeff (see box) can try out the new words he's learning, not by memorizing, but by *using* them in conversation—even with friends or family who don't know Spanish! He can speak or write in English and substitute one of his new Spanish words when appropriate. When he knows more Spanish, he can include a sentence in Spanish while he's speaking or writing in English. He can also try to become more involved with Spanish by watching a Spanish TV show, listening to a Spanish radio program, or looking at a Spanish newspaper.

LONG AND SHORT MEMORY

There are basically two different kinds of remembering: long-term and short-term. To better understand the difference, think of your brain as a parking facility. One part of it specializes in "parking" new information for only a few days. If the new information is reinforced, it gets shifted to long-term parking. Think of the long-term parking lot as your "grandmother" memory, because that's where emotional memories are stored, perhaps like the one you have of yourself as a child with your grandmother.

The only memory that really sticks with you is long-term memory. If you want to learn something at the beginning of the semester and still be able to remember that information for the final exam, you will have to move it from short-term memory to long-term memory. On the other hand, some things belong in short-term memory; they would just clutter up the long-term side. You may memorize a friend's phone number, for instance, just long enough to get to someplace where you can write it down.

Some people are very good at remembering things they learn right away. Others are better at remembering things they learned a long time ago. Which are you? Whichever you are, you may want to use your learning style to practice on the other. Below are some suggestions; you'll probably come up with more on your own or find that a combination of a few works best for you.

REMEMBERING THINGS YOU JUST LEARNED

Be prepared! Whatever you use to write your notes in, carry it with you!

Notebooks

Carry a small notebook with you and write down what you just learned. Your reading log will work for this purpose. You might want to create one section for pre-reading and questions and another for things you want to learn.

Address Books

Use an address book to create your own categories in alphabetical order. Get yourself an inexpensive address book and use it as a do-it-yourself dictionary. Write in unfamiliar words as you come across them, along with your own meaning and, perhaps, a definition you looked up in a dictionary. You could also use an address book to keep track of A–Z ideas as you prepare for an examination or paper.

Index Cards

Jot down anything you want to remember—French vocabulary, chemistry terms, mathematical equations, whatever—each on its own card.

Make sure you add your own explanation—if it's a vocabulary word, also write a sentence using the word. You can use different colored cards to designate different categories. For example, French vocabulary cards could have verbs in green and nouns in purple. Or, if you're focusing on spelling, different colored inks on the same card could designate different sounds within a word. Colors can be used to create order and help you remember new material.

Repeat It
Repeat what you just learned over and over in your head. Put it on tape and listen to it often.

Visualize It
Imagine a silly picture using what you just learned. Draw the picture in a small notebook or on an index card.

Expand It
Imagine what came before and what might come after what you just learned. Write, draw, or list what you imagined in a small notebook or on an index card.

REMEMBERING THINGS YOU LEARNED BEFORE
You might find that when you see or hear something similar to what you think you've forgotten, it comes back to you. Your memory was triggered by something.

The only way you'll find out what triggers your memory is to try different strategies for remembering. You can begin by continuing to do any (or any combination) of the things in the list above that work for you. You can also:

- **Draw charts**. Make each one a category of your design. As you learn something new in each category—or remember something from the past—add it to the chart. Look at it frequently.

- **Make audiotapes.** As you learn something new—or remember-something from the past—talk about it into an audiotape. Use different tapes for different subjects. Color-code tape labels to keep the categories separate. Play back the tapes frequently.

- **Prepare index cards**. Keep your notes on 3x5 cards. Experiment with different labels and ink colors to organize by subject. Store cards by categories and review them frequently. If you've also recorded audiotapes for the material, store the cards with the tapes in shoeboxes with color-coded labels.

- **Create timelines**. In a world history class, for example, you could put large sheets of paper on your bedroom wall to begin timelines. Since you're studying different countries during similar time periods, you could write each country's timeline in a different color. Use the same colors to make notes of events and people in those countries. Or maybe you could designate a different color for each era; that way you could keep track of what was happening when. If you're using tapes, you can similarly categorize by having one tape for each country or one for each century.

REINFORCEMENTS ARE COMING!

When you pack a heavy bag of groceries, you double up on bags to ensure that the contents stay inside. In the same way, your memory needs reinforcement to hold on to, or remember, a great deal of information. There are many ways you can make something you've learned hold in your memory.

Keep in mind your learning styles:

- **Use it**. If it's a new word or new idea, use it with friends and family. Keep using it!

- **Think about it**. Think about what the new material means to you, and to what you have learned in the past. *How* you think about it depends on what works best for you. This might mean making pictures in your head as you think about your instructor's words or putting the new material in a kind of order.

- **See it**. Write the word you want to remember and its definition in big letters on a sheet of paper. Make several copies. Put them where you're sure to notice them—on your bedroom and/or bathroom mirror, on the refrigerator, next to the telephone. Experiment with different colored markers and paper to see which works best for you.

- **Hear it**. Talk about the new material (even to yourself), read aloud, listen to tapes of a lecture or of yourself reading notes or a text.

THE PAUSE THAT REFRESHES

After you learn something new, you need "sink-in" time. Pause. Think about what you read, who you met, what you heard, what you saw.

Think of one thing you learned this week. It could be something you learned at work, at home, on your own, or with friends. Take a piece of paper, and write your answers to these questions:

- What was it I learned?
- How did I learn it?
- What did I get out of learning it? How will it be useful to me?

You just made the memory of what you learned much stronger. By thinking and writing about it, you're more likely to remember it.

HERE'S LOOKING AT YOU! USING REFLECTION

When you stand in front of a mirror, there are two of you—the real you, and your mirror image. By reflecting the real you, the mirror lets you see yourself in a way that you wouldn't be able to see otherwise. You see all of yourself head on; you see yourself more clearly.

When you think back on something, you're reflecting. You're "seeing" it more clearly. When you asked yourself the questions above, as you were pausing to let what you learned sink in, you were reflecting. Every time you reflect on what you've learned, you reinforce that memory.

OLD NEWS IS GOOD NEWS

Before you go on to something new, review what you know already. You'll be reinforcing what you've learned and making it easier to find connections with what you are about to learn.

Jeff, who we met at the beginning of this chapter, learned how to study more thoroughly. He found the more he used his Spanish—talking to the mirror, singing in the shower, listening to a Spanish-speaking radio station—the more the words sunk in. He found if he didn't use a word for a while, it was easy to forget it, no matter how strongly he felt he had learned it at the time.

WRITE ON!

Whatever your learning style, you're more likely to remember what you are learning if you write about it. (You may want to review Chapter 7, "Knowing What You Know.")

REWRITE CLASS NOTES

This can make the notes easier to read—and easier for you to remember them. This also gives you a chance to reorganize the notes so what's important to you will stand out. You might want to use colored markers for certain sections.

BE A COPY CAT

If you are learning something complex from a pamphlet or book, choose a few paragraphs you feel are most important. Copy them exactly. Then read them out loud. Copy them a second time, and then read them aloud again. Copy a third time, read aloud a third time. If you are still feeling challenged by the material, continue copying and reading aloud. This really works!

WRITE AS YOU STUDY

Each time you review your reading log, class notes, or a text, you probably see something a little differently than the time before. This is because you're getting more involved with what you're learning. Write down your more experienced viewpoints. Write how you feel about the material now, and see the progress you make with each study session.

WRITE AFTER STUDYING

Without looking at your notes or text, write what you got out of studying *this time*. Also write *how* you studied, how you used your learning styles. You'll find the more aware you are of what you do, the more likely you'll be successful at getting material to stick in your memory.

USING YOUR LEARNING STYLES AS YOU STUDY

IF YOU LEARN BEST BY HEARING

Read aloud (softly, if you're around others). Also, try using a tape recorder by recording your own notes from class and from your reading logs. Play the tape back whenever you can, when it won't disturb others. In a lecture class, many instructors will permit you to bring a recorder. If you learn best by hearing, you might find you get more out of *not* taking notes during a lecture, but by focusing instead on what you're hearing. Let your tape recorder record the lecture so you can review it , or parts of it, later.

IF YOU LEARN BEST BY SEEING

Write. Take notes in all classes, even when it's a class discussion. If something unusual happens—someone had a sneezing fit and the instructor had to stop talking—write that down, too. The unusual often helps trigger details later. If your company or school has a film library, you might want to see if what you've read about is available on film. For instance, films have been made about how to build things, conduct science experiments, and manage people. Many stories and novels have also been made into films.

IF YOU LEARN BEST BY DOING

Role play. Act out what you've learned. Nobody's watching—your character can even be a machine, if that's what you're learning about. You might also try reading and writing while walking. Some people who learn best by doing or moving find they think more clearly when they are moving. Try it!

IF YOU LEARN BEST BY USING IMAGES

Pay attention to the "movie" in your head. Draw pictures that come to mind in the margins of your own texts, or in your notebook.

IF YOU LEARN BEST BY USING ORDER

Make a list or chart. This can be of words, phrases, or questions. Outlines probably come easily to you and help align your thinking as you review old material and add new information.

(You may also want to review Chapters 2 through 5 on learning styles. See, too, Chapters 12 through 14 on getting the most from the classroom.)

IN SHORT

Getting new information to stay in your memory means finding something familiar, or unusual, in what you are learning and using your learning style to make connections. It's important to stop and reflect on what you learned, and to *use* it as often as you can.

Practice Tip

Twenty minutes or so before you go to sleep tonight, read over (or listen to) something you want to remember. Tomorrow morning, read or listen to the same thing again.

CHAPTER | 12

You are "reading with
your ears" when you
listen to a lecture. To get
the most out of the
lecture, take time to
think about what
will be covered before the
speaker begins. Take
careful notes, jot down
questions that come to you,
and summarize the lecture
in your own
words afterwards.

GETTING THE MOST FROM A LECTURE

What is a lecture? Quite simply, a lecture is a talk by one person. Lectures have been used in the classroom since medieval times, when books were scarce. At that time, a lecture was usually an instructor reading from the only book available, which was usually handwritten, since the printing press had yet to be invented. Today, sometimes lectures are read from books or notes, but often the teacher simply speaks about a subject, perhaps referring to a book or notes occasionally. Some teachers combine lecture with discussion groups; some only lecture. Your job as a student in a lecture situation is to be an active listener. You want to become involved with what you're hearing.

BEFORE THE LECTURE

In any class, it's a good idea to get the phone numbers of at least two of your classmates. Then, if you should be ill, you'll have fellow students to call to find out what you missed. They might let you copy their notes or their audiotape of a lecture. If you want to study together—even if it's over the phone—or check information, you have potential study buddies. There's more to come on this in Chapter 16, "Working with a Study Buddy."

PREPARING FOR THE LECTURE CLASS

Many schools and companies have lecture halls that can accommodate fifty or more students. Seats may or may not be assigned. Before you attend class, you can probably find out from the department or office sponsoring the class if you may choose your seat. If so, *be early!* Seats up front and along the aisles go quickly. Most lecturers permit tape recorders, but ask for permission first. Whether you learn best by hearing or seeing, it's a good idea to take advantage of a tape recorder. Especially in a large class with many distractions, it's easy to miss something that is said.

What's in a Title?

You'll probably be given the title of the lecture or the title of a reading that the lecture is based on. Get yourself tuned up for that lecture by playing a little guessing game beforehand:

- What do you think the lecture will be about?
- What do you know about the topic already—and what don't you?
- How will knowing more about the subject enhance your understanding of the class, or your knowledge in general?

Write in a notebook or record on tape whatever the title of the lecture brings to mind. Write what questions you expect the lecture to answer, based on what you think about the title. Now that you've guessed what the lecture is about—you're ready to listen!

Is There an Assignment? Do It!

If the lecture is based on an assignment, such as a reading, it's important to have this done—and understood—before the lecture, so you'll know what the lecturer is talking about. Write down any questions that come to mind while you do the assignment, ones that you hope the instructor will answer in the lecture.

MAKING SENSE OF THE LECTURE
QUESTIONS, QUESTIONS

Some instructors permit students to raise their hands and ask questions during a lecture. Others want to wait until the end of the lecture for questions. Either way, write down your questions as they come to mind. Questions can evaporate unless they're on paper, even if you'll be asking them soon.

Coming up with questions also helps you understand the lecture. For instance, you might be thinking to yourself, "I'm not sure what he's talking about right now. I can't seem to connect it with what he said a moment ago." That's a legitimate question! So you can ask: "I'm having trouble connecting what you just said with what you were talking about before. Would you explain the connection for me?"

It's important to speak up! If you have a question, others are probably thinking the same thing. You feel more involved when you participate—and you are getting more out of what you're learning. Even in lecture classes, instructors often notice—and appreciate—students willing to participate by asking questions. Sometimes the instructor is so familiar with the material that he or she forgets others need more explanation. In this sense, *you're* helping the teacher teach!

TAKING NOTES

You'll get more out of note taking if you're guided by your learning style. (You may want to review Chapters 2 through 5 on learning styles.)

If You Learn Best by Hearing

Some people who learn best by hearing find that taking notes while they're listening distracts them from what they're hearing. To test this, try both versions of the practice tip at the end of this chapter. Listen to a talk show *without* taking notes, then, on another day, listen to a talk show *with* taking notes. Decide which worked better for you. Either way, writing down questions that come to mind—or even key words that will remind you of the question—might be necessary to help you hold on to the question.

If You Learn Best by Seeing

You need to "see" while you listen. Write or draw pictures of what the lecturer is talking about. If the lecturer switches back and forth between topics, try using different colored markers to denote the different topics. If you don't have time to do this while the lecture is going on, you can do it when you go over your notes after class.

If You Learn Best by Using Images

You need to have pictures come to mind while you listen. Write or draw pictures of what the lecturer is saying. For your images to make sense, remember to think about the order of events, too! Numbering your pictures or using different colors to show you their order might help.

If You Learn Best by Using Order

You need to feel a clear order of events while you listen. Make a list or draw a timeline of what the lecturer is saying. Remember to keep track of images, too. Perhaps drawing images on your timeline would be useful.

If You Learn Best by Doing

You need to get a sense of experiencing what is being talked about. You might need to try different ways to do this, both for *doing* and for *moving*. For doing, you could pretend you're a reporter for a magazine on the subject of the lecture and you need to take careful notes so your readers will have an accurate understanding of the subject. For moving, you might find that you stay focused best by writing down as much of what the lecturer is saying as you can, and/or gently tapping your foot or finger to the lecturer's rhythm of speech. Just do it so gently that you don't disturb others around you.

On the other hand, some people who learn best by doing find that the simple act of taking notes is enough *doing* for them. You may not need to refer to your notes very often after the lecture (once you've gotten them in order, that is). The simple act of writing down the ideas helps you remember them.

Try the different ways of listening described above to see which best helps you listen attentively. Practice them in turn as you listen to a radio talk show!

REFLECTION AFTER THE LECTURE

Why do you look into a mirror more than once? What do you see that you haven't seen before? You have the same face—the same configuration of eyes, nose, mouth. What's different each time you look? Is there more sparkle in your eyes? Less color in your cheeks? A wrinkle on your brow?

When you reflect, you look back on something. Sometimes, on taking a second look, you realize something you hadn't noticed before. Reflecting also helps you remember what happened. The same way you look into a mirror to make sure the part in your hair is straight, or your tie knot is tidy, you think back on a lecture to see if everything is in order in your mind, that all the information falls into place.

Start by considering the questions you wrote (or recorded) before the lecture began. Were any of them answered during the lecture? How did your anticipation of the lecture, based on its title, compare with what was actually said? If you're left with questions, try to find the answers by reflecting on what you learned, or by speaking with the professor.

WRITE OR DRAW A SUMMARY

Things make sense to you, or "stick" with you, when you're an involved learner. You're able to connect what's new to what you already know. You find that your questions now have answers. Pictures come to mind and the order of events is clearer than before.

Now, while it's still fresh in your mind, you need to put together a complete picture of what you heard in the lecture. You need to make a summary for yourself. In this case, the summary is a condensed version of the whole lecture. You can go about this in a variety of ways. You can write it in your notebook, draw a cartoon about it, or speak your thoughts into a recorder. Any of these methods lets you refer back for a quick review and helps you remember key ideas.

The summary can be a couple of sentences for starters. Add on to it as more thoughts come to mind. You might want to have two summaries: a short one to remind you of what happened, which you can write in the top margin of your notebook or on the label of your audiotape; and a longer one that includes any details that come to mind. Your notes, after all, may be several pages in no particular order. Now is the time to make sense of them. To help you with this, you may want to review Chapter 11, "Remembering What You've Learned."

Using Notes to Help You Remember

The more you go back to your notes, adding on to them any connections or questions and answers that come to mind, the greater chance you'll have of remembering the material. Re-writing notes can help you put them in an order that makes more sense to you. If you learn better by images, re-writing can help you connect your images more clearly. If you learn better by order, re-writing, perhaps in an outline form, can assist you in understanding—and remembering—more of what you've heard.

Taking notes from your audiotape as you re-listen can help you focus on what you're hearing. The more you listen, writing down additional questions and ideas as they come to mind, the more you'll get out of your tape. Treat your taped lecture the same way you would treat a favorite album: listen to it over and over again.

Since everyone learns differently, keep reminding yourself of what works for *you*. You will be more likely to repeat your success in getting a lot out of the lecture if you also figure out and write down *why* it was a success.

In Short

Before a lecture begins, pre-read by anticipating what it will be about. During the lecture, write questions as they come to mind. Then ask them of the lecturer. Use your learning style—take notes if you learn best by seeing, focus on listening if you learn best by hearing. After the lecture, write a summary of what it was about and its value to you.

Practice Tips

Listen to a Radio Talk Show. Check radio listings in your newspaper to find a program that interests you. Get ready by writing out what you expect the program to be about. Then write down questions you expect the program to answer.

- **If you learn best by hearing**: Focus on *hearing* the program. As soon as it's over, write down or draw a comic strip of what it was about.

- **If you learn best by seeing**: Take notes or draw as you listen. If other questions come to mind, write them down. Write or draw a summary of the talk.

Include in your reflections:

- Which of your questions were answered?
- What helped you focus on the talk?
- What helped you write your reflections?

Try It in a Phone Conversation. The next time you're talking on the telephone, write down what the other person is saying. How did that help you remember later on what the person said?

CHAPTER | 13

A lot happens in class participation. You have to be on your toes—listening to the lecture and to other students, putting together what you hear with what you know about the subject, and getting ready to volunteer or be called upon to speak. It sounds like a lot of work, but getting involved is actually quite enjoyable and stimulating. The more active you are in class discussion, the more you'll feel a part of the class and the more you'll get out of it.

GETTING THE MOST FROM CLASS PARTICIPATION

Some teachers simply lecture for the whole class period, every class period. Other teachers, though, like to use class participation for all or part of their instruction. Many students don't like class participation, either because they'd rather hear what the teacher has to say than what their fellow students think, or because they just don't want to speak in class.

(To get the most from this chapter, you may wish to review Chapter 3, "Looking and Listening," Chapter 9, "Getting Involved," and Chapter 12, "Getting the Most from a Lecture.")

Getting Around Shyness

Janine enjoyed the lectures in her nursing class. She just didn't want to be called on or pressured to volunteer. She'd cringe just before the student comment period that ended every class. She tried to slide down in her seat so she wouldn't be called on. She kept her eyes on her notebook. Her instructor saw what was happening and finally asked Janine to stay after class for a few minutes one day. She explained to Janine that she had set up the class so that students would get more out of it by actively taking part, and Janine wasn't taking advantage of that opportunity. Janine wasn't surprised to hear the teacher's comments; she knew she had to get over her shyness if she wanted to get the most out of the course.

Classes where professors encourage students to engage in discussion have many advantages over straight lecture courses. If you're one of those people who doesn't like class participation, consider the following benefits that don't come with a lecture course. A class in which you speak as well as listen is more *active* than a class in which you just listen. When you learn by doing, you are really *learning*. When you're *involved*, you're having a different experience than if you're just sitting there. You're more apt to pay attention, remember, and get real meaning out of the class. In fact, being involved can even make you excited about what you're studying!

ACTIVE LISTENING

As you know by now, people listen and retain what they hear in different ways. How well you use your learning style in a class of participating students can make a great deal of difference in how much you learn and remember.

- **If you learn best by seeing:** You'll probably find an active class helps you keep better tabs on what you're hearing. There's more reinforcement for what's been said, with students (including you!) asking questions and offering comments. Taking careful and frequent notes will give you something to see—and re-reading them will help you recall the class. Remember, about half of everybody learns better by seeing. You're not alone in working to make sense-of what you hear!

- **If you learn best by hearing:** Much depends on the kind of memory you have. Some hearing-learners can hold onto information for a whole class period, writing their notes *after* class. Others find writing down some cues about what happened right away, as it happens, helps them remember later.

- **If you learn best using images:** Draw pictures of the ideas, people, and images that come from what you hear, connecting pictures to show the influence of one on another and the relationships between them.

- **If you learn best using order:** Make a list of ideas, events, even of the other students and what they said that you find significant.

- **If you learn best through doing:** Talk a lot. Use hand gestures if this helps you get your ideas flowing. While you're listening, put yourself in the mind-set of somebody connected with the subject at hand and imagine what you'd be thinking, feeling and doing; who'd you be interacting with; and so on.

Janine (see box) found that if she pretended she was in a clinic, and her classmates and instructor were co-workers, it was easier for her to pay attention during discussion time.

MAKE ASSOCIATIONS

Another way to keep track of what's being said is to *associate*. Some clever teachers will pause or do something unusual after something important has been said—maybe stamp a foot or spin around. But, sometimes something unusual happens by itself: a woman has a sneezing fit just after the function of the thigh-bone is explained, for example. When things like this happen in the classroom, you're likely to remember that sneeze and also facts about the thigh bone. That's because people are apt to remember the unusual.

Ask If You Can't Hear

After her talk with her teacher and a little practice at home, Janine was becoming more comfortable with the participation part of class. She learned to say things like, "Excuse me, I can't hear you. Please repeat what you said," and, "I'm having trouble understanding what you just said. Do you mean . . .?" She found the more she helped others make themselves understood, the more she was getting out of the class—she discovered she was interested in what the other students had to say.

Maybe you know how to help others listen to you, but some of them aren't helping you listen to them. You have a right to know what's being said. It's your job to tell someone if they're not loud enough, or if you're confused by what they're saying.

PUTTING IT ALL TOGETHER

You've listened carefully, but how can you make sense of what really matters and what doesn't, of what's valuable to your learning and what is just peripheral information that doesn't contribute anything important to your study? And how do you combine the instructor's lecture with student comments to keep track of what's happening in this class? How can you put it all together?

This is where active learning can really help. Take notes to keep track of the exchange of ideas taking place in class. Use your learning style—drawing, making lists, whatever works for you. If you're a strong literal and/or visual learner, try numbering your notes or drawing lines connecting common themes in what you've written. This will help give you an idea of the direction that the instructor-student dialogue is going. Then you'll be prepared to ask informed questions!

PARTICIPATING
GETTING THE GUMPTION TO SPEAK

Usually people are anxious about speaking in class because they're afraid they'll make some kind of mistake. Aside from the fact that some teachers require participation, and grade accordingly, once you accept yourself as a bona fide class member—and an appreciated contributor—you'll not only get more out of class, you'll feel good, too.

You're Doing It Already

When you speak at the dinner table, asking family or friends about their day, chatting comfortably, *contributing* to what's being talked about, you're in an active learning situation. Think of all the practice you've had already!

Get Comfortable to Share Experiences

Think of your classmates as friends or co-workers. You're not on the stage of Carnegie Hall. You're in room 2G-432, Anatomy Class.

And remember, you have something important to say that *only you can say*. Only you think and feel like you. Everyone in the class may have read the same text and come to similar conclusions, but only you have had your experience. When you share your experience with others, you're helping them keep an open mind.

Making Yourself Heard

OK, now you'll talk. But you're afraid it won't come out right, that you'll be misunderstood, or that no one will listen. Consider the following advice.

Relax

Nervous? You're not alone. Take a few minutes before class to close your eyes and imagine a quiet place. Take a few deep breaths—inhale for four counts, then exhale for four counts. Try to create this same calm feeling when you're in class with your hand raised. When it's your turn to speak, take it slow, and bring your voice down a little. You'll feel less nervous automatically. (There's more on keeping calm in Chapter 1, "Getting Started.")

Getting It Out

Think out what you want to say before you say it. Writing it out or making a list helps, too. You might find after you've begun to speak, more ideas come to you—keep talking!

Tongue-Tied?

When people who stutter are interviewed on the radio, they stutter less or not at all. If stuttering is a problem for you, talk to your instructor. Let him or her know your situation; maybe this will help you feel more comfortable. You might find that in the somewhat public situation of class, you stutter less.

Help Them Listen

Wait until someone has finished speaking before beginning to speak. You'll get more respect—and better listeners when you do speak. If you had to wait awhile to speak, and the topic shifted a little, help the class understand your meaning by beginning with, "I want to go back to what we were talking about before. . . ."

The clearer you are, the less questions others will have in their heads and the easier it will be for them to attentively listen to you.

Long-Winded?

Being long-winded often means wanting attention. Participating in class means getting attention, but you want to make sure you're not demanding more than your share.

Practice at home. Think of something that would be appropriate to say in class. Write it down to hold on to the complete idea. Set a kitchen timer for 30 seconds. If you're still talking, go back to what you wrote. Did you add to it as you spoke? Or did you write more than would be appropriate to say at one time? Reward yourself for every time you control the amount of time you speak.

To avoid a mood where you feel the need to have all eyes on you for an unfair amount of time, try giving yourself a reward before class. Have a good meal or snack, or take a walk. Even giving yourself extra time to get to class can be a reward.

STICKY SITUATIONS
Being Nervous

You're nervous, and the instructor asks you to stand up or (gulp!) stand in the front of the class to give your presentation. Depending on just how nervous you are, try looking at a supportive friend. Alternatively, you can look over the tops of the heads of your classmates to the back of the room. You'll find avoiding eye contact helpful because you don't feel so much like you're being examined.

Forgetting What You Were Going to Say

You started to speak, then forgot what you were going to say. You can avoid this in the future by writing your comment on paper as soon as it comes to you. If you're pressed for time, list key words. If you're really pressed for time—no time to write, that is—try chanting the key words over in your head, or designating different fingers for each of your key words and holding onto those fingers. If your mind does go blank, just say, "I forgot what I was going to say." This happens to *everybody* at some time or other.

QUESTIONS AND ANSWERS
Asking Questions

All instructors encourage questions. If you have a question, chances are other students do, too. Check with your instructor if questions are preferred during class, or saved for after class. It's a good idea to write down questions as they come to mind, particularly if your instructor is lecturing and prefers questions *after* the lecture. Also, once you have your question in writing, you can re-word it to make it clearer. Try to stick to the point.

Responding to Questions

In some classes, the instructor will pose questions for students to answer, or the instructor will encourage other students to answer student questions.

Plan in advance. *Before* class begins, review your notes of the last class. Review any required reading, too. Pretend you're the instructor. Come up with questions. Then come up with your answers. Make sure you have proof—from your reading—of your answers. Even if the questions you raised are different from the questions that occur in the classroom, your practice will help you become familiar with the material.

IN SHORT

You make the most of your learning when you're involved, and many classes expect you to get involved through some kind of class participation. Often this is done by encouraging students to share their comments and questions during a lecture or immediately after it. Keep notes of what the instructor and your classmates say. Get more out of listening by asking questions. Help others hear what you have to say by speaking up and being informed and prepared.

The next chapter shows you how to deal with a different kind of active classroom, one that uses small-group discussion.

Practice Tip

The next time you're with a group of friends, family members, or coworkers, take notes to keep track of the discussion and to help you decide what you want to say before you speak. If they ask why you're taking notes, simply tell them the truth—that you're practicing for class—it'll give them something to talk about!

CHAPTER | 14

In small discussion groups, everyone takes turns giving their impressions and opinions about a chosen subject. Members listen to each other, think about how they agree and disagree with others' comments, and, depending upon the assignment, complete a project or come to a consensus.

GETTING THE MOST FROM A CLASS DISCUSSION GROUP

Small discussion groups are a popular way of getting students actively involved in the study topic. Usually you'll break into groups of three to eight people. Often, you wind up in a group with those sitting near you, but sometimes a teacher wants to arrange the groups in a specific way. He might group people who have something in common, such as interests, or age, or both. Or he may intentionally combine people of different interests and ages so that each group represents the overall mix of the class. Usually the groups are given a specific assignment. They might, for instance, be asked to answer questions, debate an issue, work on an experiment, or prepare a short class presentation. Everyone is encouraged to participate.

WHY WORK IN GROUPS?

When you work with other students in a group, you're becoming more responsible for your own learning because *your* voice is being heard, not just the instructor's. This is an easy and comfortable way to get to know students in your class. You'll also see that not only are "two heads better than one," but three or four contribute even more! To get ready for such interaction, you may want to review Chapter 16, "Working With a Study Buddy."

TYPES OF GROUP ASSIGNMENTS

Instructors set up groups and give group assignments for different reasons. Your group may be asked to:

- Discuss something you recently learned, either through reading or a lecture, to help you solidify what you know and find out what you still have questions about.
- Do a kind of group pre-reading, exploring a topic you have not yet learned by finding connections with topics you've already learned.
- Perform a specific task, like dissecting a frog in biology class.
- Respond to a written or oral contribution by each group member. For instance, in a writing class, each member of the group might read his or her essay aloud so that other group members can discuss what's good and what needs improvement.

TYPES OF GROUP STRUCTURES

There are different ways for a group to be organized. Yours might be structured along these lines:

- A leader or timekeeper makes sure each person speaks within a time limit.
- A recorder or secretary writes down what each person says and reads back the notes to the group after everyone has spoken.

- A reporter tells the class what the group discovered or decided in its discussion.

The instructor may have one person fulfill all these roles, rotating the position with each class meeting.

Other groups are much less formal. Your instructor may not give you any instructions at all about who should do what, as long as your group accomplishes the work it's assigned. You'll probably find in such cases one or two students naturally take the role of leader. Your group may want to choose someone to take group notes. It's only fair to try to pass these roles around rather than having one or two people do all the work all the time.

HOW TO MAKE YOUR GROUP WORK

As the group solves a problem or comes to a conclusion, every person needs to know how each other member thinks and feels. In order to accomplish this, it's important to follow some basic rules.

GROUP ETIQUETTE

Be Prepared

Keep up with your assignments. Your group relies on each member's opinions and interpretations.

Speak When It's Your Turn

If you're nervous about speaking, take a deep breath. Remind yourself you're with students who are very similar to you—and who are probably as nervous as you are. The more you speak, the less nervous you'll be. Go back to Chapter 13, "Getting the Most from Class Participation," for tips on overcoming stage fright when you speak in your group.

Keep Within the Time Limit

Stay within your time limit, if one is assigned. If not, it's simply good manners to show consideration and only use your share of the discussion time. This is the only way everyone can get to speak. Also, there has to be time at the end of the discussion for the group to come to a conclusion. If it's difficult for you to stop talking, try saying what's most important first.

Pay Attention

Listen carefully when it's someone else's turn. It's a good idea to take notes. With so many different ideas being talked about, this will help you to keep track of all ideas and comments.

Help Your Group Get Going

Whether your instructor has students take turns leading each group or you're all on your own, the group needs everyone to participate. Be prepared to coax someone who's shy. If someone is reluctant to speak, ask, "How do you feel about this?" or, "Do you agree with . . . ?" You might need to remind people to speak loud enough for everyone to hear.

Take Notes

Some instructors have students take turns recording the discussion and reporting to the class. Even if your group doesn't have a recorder or secretary writing down what others say, take notes of what's happening. It is also helpful to bring your own tape recorder. These tactics will help you better remember what was discussed.

TALKING IN A GROUP

Not everybody understands best by hearing. Even those that do might be distracted by what they're waiting to say, or by what they overhear other groups talking about.

Try to keep people's attention by speaking clearly. Look at the faces of your group members. Does anybody look like they're not understanding what you are saying? Clues might include a wrinkled forehead or nose, or even a blank stare. If you get such signals, try speaking more loudly. If someone still looks like they don't understand you, try repeating what you said in a different way. Ask someone, "Could you clearly hear what I said?" if there's any doubt you were understood.

LISTENING IN A GROUP

A good way to make sure you heard what the speaker wanted you to hear is to *repeat what you thought she said*. Since people think faster than they speak, there's a good chance she didn't say quite what she thought she said—or what she *meant* was different from what she said. By telling someone what you heard, you are helping avoid confusion.

If you're confused by what someone said, say what you thought you heard and follow that up with, "Is that what you meant?" If you use the exact word or phrase that your group-mate used, that will give him the sense that you understood what he said. Then you might try re-stating what he said in your own words so that you'll both know you mean the same thing.

COMING TO A CONCLUSION

After each person has spoken, the recorder reads back what each person said and the group considers how they see the same thing differently, or how they agree.

In some cases, your group might be asked to argue the matter until you come to an agreement. This is called coming to a *consensus*. This occurs when each person in the group *consents* to a certain position. Reaching consensus takes good communication skills, so be sure to listen carefully and talk using the guidelines for group etiquette above.

IN SHORT

Group discussion gets everyone involved. But in order for it to work well, each person needs to focus on the topic at hand, speak within time limits, listen carefully, and respect others' opinions. Identify what you agree with and why—and what you disagree with or are confused about and why.

Practice Tips

Polish your listening and speaking skills. The next time you're talking with someone—at the dinner table, at the water cooler, or whatever—tell her what you *thought she said* and then ask her if that was what she meant. As you are speaking, repeat a word or phrase that she used. Pay close attention to her response as you speak. If she shows signs of not hearing you or being confused, try saying what you just said in a different way. Write in your notebook what seemed to work best: How did you speak so that she understood what you meant?

Have a mini group discussion. Come up with a question from your study matter that would get a group going, something that people have opinions about or are interested in. A controversial subject is ideal here. Ask a few classmates, perhaps shortly before or after class, the question you came up with. Write in your notebook what you learned about the topic from that little discussion.

CHAPTER | 15

MAKING YOURSELF UNDERSTOOD

There are two main ways of making yourself understood in a classroom or training situation: speaking and writing. Making yourself understood boils down to focusing on what's important and then explaining it so that others can understand how you feel, what you think, and what you know.

Speaking and writing are ways of expressing yourself. When you express yourself, especially to people who don't know you, you want to be as clear as possible; this will avoid any confusion about what you think, know, or feel. The casual way you speak and write to friends can be different from the more formal way you often need to speak and write for classmates and teachers.

Speaking and writing help stimulate your thoughts. Even speaking to yourself or writing in a private journal can help you think more clearly. In these cases, it doesn't matter how it comes out; you're the only one who has to understand what you're saying. But in order to be understood by others, you need to speak and write clearly and often more formally. You want to make certain that others know what you mean.

Say It in Words

"I can't describe it," said Louie. "Can't I just show you?"

"Try again," said his computer instructor; "describe, in words, how you just did that operation." Louie was stumped. Why was it so hard to explain something he knew so much about?

TIPS FOR CONSTRUCTING A SPEECH OR PAPER

ME, MYSELF, AND I

In order to make yourself understood, say or write what matters most to *you* about a lecture, book, or article. You get your point across better when you're involved with what you're saying or writing. A good way to focus on what's important to you is to use the magic word "I," (unless, of course, an instructor tells you to avoid this pronoun in formal writing). Here are some examples: "I had a clear picture in my head where the author talked about . . ." or, "I'm confused here," or, "I felt most involved with the part on. . . ." Using your own point of view is an effective way to develop and clarify your ideas on a subject.

WHAT DO I SAY?

Hmmm, you have to come up with a topic and you're stuck. Since you want to talk about something that interests you, make a list of what you found interesting in the class. Carry the list around with you for a while and add to it as ideas come to mind. Narrow the list to three items. Then write next to each item why it interests you. Read the three reasons and choose the strongest. Voila! There's your topic.

"OK," you might say. "Now I have the topic, but I have to develop a specific focus." That's true; you're not going to be speaking all night or writing a ninety-page paper. Use the same approach you used for choosing the topic: Write quickly those things that first come to mind when you think of your topic. Now choose the thing that you like best about what you wrote. There's your focus.

QUESTIONS—ASKING AND ANSWERING

When writing an essay or paper or when preparing a speech, put yourself in the place of your reader or audience. Imagine what questions your audience might ask, and make sure the answers to these questions are covered in your speech or paper.

If it's a paper you're writing, then your reader will most likely be your teacher. What do you know about the kinds of things she wants to see in a paper? Anticipate the questions she'll be expecting you to answer. If it's a speech, the audience will probably be your teacher and your classmates. Because you're also a student, putting yourself in your classmates' place should be easy. What would you like to know about the subject? And what questions would you have about it?

WHAT DO I SAY ABOUT IT?

Remember, writing and speaking trigger your thinking. Choose your weapon!

For ideas on what to say in your speech or paper, go back to what you wrote about the topic when you were coming up with your focus. Circle your strongest ideas and cross out those things that don't support your topic. Then ask yourself questions:

- "What other details are needed for my audience to have clear pictures in their minds of what I'm talking about?" or
- "How can I make the order of the information clear to my listeners?"

You could also list what the topic makes you think of, then make sub-lists of what the items you've written down bring to mind. Or you could talk into a tape recorder, letting the ideas come as if you were talking to a friend. When you play back your recording, make note of what you liked best and why, as well as what questions came to mind.

MAKING PICTURES

Just about everyone uses imagery to some extent in making sense of what they're listening to or reading. A good way of helping your listeners use imagery is by telling a story. A small story often used by speakers to make a point is called an *anecdote*. If used well, anecdotes can get your audience involved and interested in your topic. Because anecdotes show by example or explanation, they're good devices for helping people understand what you mean. Whether you realize it or not, you're telling anecdotes all the time! In talking with friends, you easily say something like, "I remember when I . . . " or "The other day Ron said the funniest thing. . . ."

 Think of something you have recently read or listened to. What pictures came to mind? Was a story being told? Is there a little story of your own—an anecdote—that you can add to what you read or heard? Pay attention to the way authors, radio announcers, or even your best friend capture your attention with anecdotes. Try to adopt their methods.

MAKING A SPEECH

Not all instructors require you to make a speech in class, but some do. Some also might give you a choice between making a speech or writing a paper. Speeches can be written:

- As a paper, which you either read aloud, or (ideally!) use as notes and refer to when you need a reminder of what you want to say
- In outline form, which can help you keep your focus
- As notes on cards, containing key words or phrases, direct quotations, and any instructions you want to give to yourself (colored cards can help keep you focused; writing in bold black marker will make the cards easier to read).

Some instructors request a specific method of speech preparation. If you're given a choice, do what suits you. You may want to do a combination of the above—say, writing out what you want to say, then making an outline as a reminder to yourself during the speech.

Are you comfortable talking to others? Then *talk* instead of reading. You might want to work from an outline or cards. If talking in front of a group doesn't come easily to you, *read* your paper—but make it *sound* like you're talking. This comes from several practice readings of your paper.

How Do I Say It?

When speaking to an audience, you want to be heard, and you want to be listened to. You want to speak clearly and loudly enough for the people in the back row to hear you. You can practice this by opening your hand and putting it over your diaphragm, which is roughly between your navel and chest. Stand straight so you can breathe in deeply; this calms you as it helps you speak loudly. When you are speaking from your diaphragm (feel the vibrations?), the sound carries farther than when you're speaking from your throat as most people usually do. Try speaking slowly, so every word is heard. Pause after you say something important.

Give Yourself the Time It Takes

Allow plenty of time to prepare your speech—and to practice your delivery. Being unprepared for a speech isn't like being unprepared for a test; it could be a lot more embarrassing. Take days or even weeks to get ready.

Listen to Speeches

Check with your library for tapes of speeches. Tell the librarian what your interests are because it's important you listen to something you enjoy! Or listen to a speech on the radio or TV. Listen carefully, and take notes. Where and when does the speaker pause? Where and when does the speaker change her intonation or volume, speaking more loudly or softly? What kind of impact does this have on you as listener?

Get Started

Begin by having a friend or family member listen to you talk about your topic. Ask him what he liked best, and what he would like to hear more of. You can also practice in front of a mirror, watching how you stand and move, and noting your facial expressions. Or make an audio or videotape of yourself.

Try the speech again, after revising according to your listeners' comments and your own ideas about what needs improvement. Have your listener listen to this next version. Ask him the same questions, comparing the two versions. Be prepared to do another version. Try to get more listeners. The more practice you have, the calmer you'll feel and better you'll sound!

It's OK to have some stage fright. Actually, it's helpful. Being a little nervous gets the adrenaline going, so when you're making your speech, you're more apt to remember what you want to say and to deliver it clearly.

Get Comfortable

Think of yourself talking to a friend when you deliver your speech. Some people are comfortable looking at one person; some would rather look over the heads of the people in the room. See what works best for you.

WRITING: THE LONG AND SHORT OF IT

Some teachers might ask you to write a reflection of what you've learned at the end of class, or to keep a journal. Or you might have to write longer, more formal papers, like an essay exam or research paper.

WHEN IT'S INFORMAL—WRITING ON THE SPOT

Writing, especially informal writing in a short reflection or in a journal, is another form of talking. If you're comfortable talking, "talk" on paper. If images come to you more readily than words, describe the pictures in your head. Remember to focus on what you know best and to use the magic "I" word to keep this focus.

When you're finished writing, read your work over carefully. Make certain you said everything you wanted to say—and said it the *way* you wanted! Try reading it softly or to yourself so you can listen for anything that needs revising.

Louie, who we met at the beginning of the chapter, found that when he focused on describing the pictures in his head, his words made a lot more sense. When Louie used this tactic, the computer instructor understood exactly what he was trying to say.

WHEN IT'S FORMAL—THE ESSAY OR PAPER

Most teachers ask for some kind of formal writing, usually an essay or research paper. What's expected with this form is that your ideas be explained so that the reader is left with no confusion about the topic.

An essay is more formal than reflections, but less formal than a research paper. In an essay, you're proving what you know. (There's more about essays in Chapter 19, "Preparing for Essay Tests.")

The point of an essay is to communicate how you feel, and why you feel that way. This means backing up your feelings and opinions with facts including references to readings and lectures. One good way to make sure you include important facts like dates, names, and events is to pretend you're writing your essay for a newspaper.

For a research paper, you are expected to research a topic and write about it clearly and completely enough so that you are, in essence, teaching someone else about your topic. If your instructor assigns a research paper, she will also most likely tell you how to go about using your research in your writing. It's important that you not let the research overwhelm the task of writing: communicating with your reader.

Getting Started

If you're asked to come up with your own topic for an essay or research paper, use the tips for choosing a topic for a speech. Begin as if you were writing informally. Use your learning styles:

- Write down everything that comes to mind, then narrow down the items until you're left with one that appeals to you most.

- Talk into a tape recorder, then write what you hear when you play it back.

- Draw pictures, then describe your pictures in words.

- Make an outline or make lists.

    In doing whatever you're most comfortable with, come up with as many ideas as possible and then narrow your interests to a specific topic.

Stuck?

Have a friend act as your secretary, writing down what you say and asking you questions to keep you going.

Organizing

Even though you're using formal English, you're still, in a sense, telling a story. Stories have a beginning, middle, and end. Organize your thoughts into three groups: the introduction, body, and conclusion. Creating order early on makes for a more coherent final paper.

BE YOUR OWN EDITOR

Look at your draft with your eyes wide open. Circle what you like best, check what makes that stronger, cross out what gets in the way. Rewrite, putting the circled part first. Role-play. Pretend you're the editor of your favorite publication. Pretend somebody else wrote your draft. What questions do you have for the author? Write them down; answer them. Decide where the new information should go. Re-write, including your answers.

Another good way to edit is to turn your draft into a jigsaw puzzle. Make a copy of it to keep whole and refer to. Cut up the other version, paragraph by paragraph. Move the paragraphs around. Which way makes most sense? What do you need to add to make the meaning clearer? If you work on a computer, cutting and pasting your writing back together is easy. Separate the paragraphs with lines or spaces and read each one as a separate unit. Move paragraphs around on the screen until they're the way you want them.

You think faster than you write. When you read your paper, you're likely to remember what you were thinking. Read aloud to slow yourself down and focus more on what you see. Pay close attention to any missing words or word endings. A change of punctuation or spelling can change meaning; make sure your grammar and spelling are correct.

BE A COPY CAT

A nearly purr-fect way to improve your speaking and writing (and reading, too, actually) is to choose an article you *really* enjoyed from any newspaper or magazine. Read it aloud. Copy it, and read it again. Copy once more, and read again. The next day, choose another article and repeat. After a couple of weeks, if you do this every day, you should see a difference in the way you speak, write, and read.

IN SHORT

When you speak and write, you're communicating to others what you think and feel and what you know. To be understood, create questions about your topic and make sure that you answer those questions. In preparing a speech or writing a paper, focus on creating pictures with words and follow an order that makes sense. Answer any questions that come to mind. Use the magic word "I." Use anecdotes to help your audience understand your point and get involved in what you are saying or writing.

Practice Tips

If you're more comfortable speaking than writing, try speaking into a tape recorder. As you play it back, write down what you said. This is a good way to hear yourself speak, too.

Draw a picture of something simple. It could be a cup and saucer, a tree, anything. Then write a description of it so clearly that someone else could draw the same picture from what you wrote. Give the written description to someone; ask them to draw exactly the picture they see in their heads. Compare the new picture with the original. Write in your notebook what helped you write your description.

CHAPTER | 16

You can work with a buddy whether you are both studying the same thing or not. Your buddy can be a friend, family member, or classmate. By making yourself understood, listening carefully, and working with both your learning style and that of your partner, you'll get more out of studying. And you'll have more fun, too!

WORKING WITH A STUDY BUDDY

Studying can be nerve wracking. Maybe you've heard yourself say things like:

- "I don't remember seeing this problem before!"
- "I don't know what this means!"
- "I don't know if I'm right or not!"
- "I'm having a lot of trouble focusing."

You'll probably feel a lot less pressured if you've got someone else to work with. When you work with a partner, you have someone to bounce ideas off of, discuss things with, and ask questions. Here's how a study buddy can help:

- If you're working on the same problem, one of you might know the answer and can help the other; if neither of you knows it, you can figure it out together.
- If you're not working on the same thing, your partner can ask you questions to help you focus your studying. He can also quiz you on the material and help you pinpoint your weak areas. And of course, you can do the same for him!

Two Heads Are Better Than One

Jack: "What a waste of time. I don't know why the sociology instructor showed us that movie. Nothing much happened in it."

Jill: "I disagree. I was really impressed by the way the people of the village stuck together and the way they treated their children."

Jack: "That's true. I was surprised. You'd think those kids would be spoiled by all that affection, but it was just the opposite. They really cared about each other. I guess that's why the instructor showed it. But it was still too long."

Jill: "I didn't understand the part about the government workers coming to the village. Why couldn't they just leave the villagers alone?"

Jack: "I kind of liked that part; there was more action, with the trucks coming in and the villagers protesting. I guess it had something to do with the government trying to change the economy, trying to help the villagers get regular jobs instead of digging for roots."

Jill: "I hadn't thought about that. That makes sense."

What happened here? Both Jack and Jill saw the film a little differently after reflecting and discussing. Jack began to make more sense of the human issues in the film and Jill began to make more sense of the political ones. By working together, they made sense of something that was puzzling at first. They figured out much more than they would have working separately.

GETTING STARTED

You may not be aware of it, but you already know how to work with a study buddy. Whenever you discuss a film, newspaper or magazine article, or event with a friend, you're "working" with a buddy. If you saw the film or read the article, your friend might ask, "What did you think about it?" maybe adding, "I heard it was . . ." or, "I've been meaning to see it myself." Your friend is *helping you remember* what you saw, heard, or read by asking you that general question.

As you think back on the film or event to tell your friend, you might think about it a little differently than you did when you saw it. Since your subconscious has had some time to pull it together, you're more apt to have a clearer opinion of it now. Your modified thoughts were triggered by your friend's questions.

If the two of you had experienced the same thing, you would be prompting each other, even if you had very different reactions. The idea of working with a buddy isn't to change someone's mind, but to help that person be more aware of what they're really feeling and thinking.

FINDING A STUDY BUDDY

You probably know at least one person in your class. And most likely you have some classmates' phone numbers in case you miss a class and need to borrow notes or be filled in on what happened. You could ask one of these people to study with you.

But maybe you're not in a class. Maybe you're preparing for a test you have to take on your own, like a civil service or certification exam. Or maybe your schedule doesn't match any of your classmates'. In that case, look to a friend, coworker, or family member who you think would be willing to work with you.

Finding the *Right* Study Buddy

Whomever you choose, you want to work with someone who:

- You're comfortable with
- Is responsible: who will keep study appointments, who takes learning seriously—and takes you seriously

Friend or Not?

You may think that your best friend or closest family member will be your best study buddy, and that can be true *some of the time*. For instance, if you're terribly intimidated by the material you're studying and your best friend or younger sister is the kind of person who gives you the confidence you need to do well, this person may indeed be the best study buddy you could possibly have.

But there are drawbacks to working with someone you know well. You might be tempted to spend your study sessions talking about things other than the topic at hand; you might not get much studying done! If you study with someone you barely know, you have less to talk about and are more likely to stay focused on the study material. Whoever you decide to work with, make sure you use study sessions for their purpose: to learn the material, prepare for a test, or complete an assignment.

Using Learning Styles

When you're working on a project, which is easier for you? Starting it, developing it after it's started, or bringing it to a close and finishing it up? What's more comfortable for you may be connected with your learning style. Those who learn best by doing often find starting comes easily to them. People who like to use images are often adept at "keeping the ball rolling"—developing ideas after a project's begun. Sequential learners are often naturals for developing and completing a project on time.

It's not a bad idea, then, to try to find a study buddy whose learning style is different from your own. If you're good at starting projects but lose steam once things are underway, wouldn't it be nice to have a study buddy who will help you keep it going and get it done by the deadline?

SETTING UP A TIME AND PLACE

It's important for you and your study buddy to meet fairly regularly. Try an hour a week to start. Decide together what days of the week and times are best for you both.

Decide where you'd like to meet. You could take turns going to each other's home. Some libraries have meeting rooms that you can reserve ahead of time; such neutral territory might be the ideal place to keep you focused. Does your place of work permit after-hours meetings? Is there a quiet coffee shop nearby? You want a place that's free of distraction and convenient for both of you.

GETTING THE MOST FROM YOUR STUDY BUDDY

Here are some tips for how you and your study buddy can work together.

SET AN AGENDA

The first thing you and your study buddy have to decide is how long your session will be and what you want to cover in that time. Be realistic when you do this; don't try to cover fifty pages of your textbook in an hour. You may also want to set aside specific portions of your time for special purposes, such as:

- **At the start:** Five minutes at the beginning for sharing news of the day or airing complaints. If you set aside a specific time period for talking about how yesterday's math test was or what a lousy day you had, you won't be tempted to spend any more time on it during the rest of your session.
- **At the end:** Five to ten minutes at the end for reviewing what you've just learned. Spending time reviewing will help you solidify what you learned and clarify what you still need to work on.

USE YOUR TIME TOGETHER WELL

Here are some things you and your study buddy can do to help each other understand the material:

- Explain to each other what you already know.
- Help each other find out what you don't know.
- Ask each other questions.
- Help each other find the answers.
- Make connections between what you've just learned and what you already know.
- Give feedback in preparation for an essay or in-class speech.
- Test each other on what one knows and the other doesn't. (There's more on this to come in Chapters 18 and 19 on test preparation.)

USING YOUR LEARNING STYLES

Here's how you can work awith a study buddy, depending on whether your eyes or your ears are your strong suit.

- **If you learn best by seeing:** As a visual learner, you might have trouble learning when you have to use your ears. Keep notes diligently. When your study buddy makes an interesting point, write it down. Keeping a log of study sessions will help refresh your memory before a test.
- **If you learn best by hearing:** Maybe you think more clearly when speaking. Ask your study buddy to act as your secretary. Dictate to her what you want to say in the written assignment you have to complete. It's important that she write down exactly what you say.

When You're Both Studying the Same Thing

There's a lot of comfort in working with someone who's going through the same thing you are! Jack, who we met in the beginning of the chapter, resented watching the film, yet, after discussing it with his study buddy, Jill, he came to a deeper understanding of it.

When you try to understand someone else's point of view, you become more open to new ideas. And when you explain your own point of view to someone else, you clarify it in your mind.

When You're Not Studying the Same Thing

There's a big advantage to you if your partner is *not* reading the same thing you are, because he or she is then in a better position to ask pointed questions about your study material. You're also compelled to give more complete answers because you can't assume your partner knows anything about the reading. This in turn gets you to better understand what you've read, and it helps you write more clearly about the reading.

If Jill had not seen the sociology film, she could have asked, "What was it about? What was useful about it?" and so on. Then Jack would have had to think carefully and explain it to her in detail.

GROUND RULES FOR STUDYING TOGETHER

Keep your heads clear and cool by showing respect for each other. You can do this when you:

- Appreciate each other's learning styles.
- Start with a positive point before criticizing.
- Use sensitive talk; be aware of each other's needs and perspectives; keep open minds.
- Listen attentively.

APPRECIATE EACH OTHER'S LEARNING STYLES

To make the most of studying together, you both need to know what works for the other. Tell your buddy about your learning style. Tell her what you need and encourage your buddy to do the same with you. After all, you've both got the same goal: to learn what you're studying. You both want to get the most out of these sessions, so be clear from the start. You'll both appreciate the other's honesty.

There's a good chance that your partner will be a different kind of learner from you, so be prepared to work with his or her style as well as yours. The most pronounced differences in learning styles are between seeing or hearing, so focus on those. Also, since you and your buddy will be working on communicating with each other, what matters most is being able to understand what your buddy says, and to make yourself understood. The following guidelines should help.

- **If you learn best by seeing:** You might need to hear things twice. Perhaps you need to ask your partner to speak more slowly or to show you something in writing.
- **If you learn best by hearing:** You might need to encourage your partner to speak more. Perhaps you need to ask your partner to read something aloud to you. Maybe it would help to hear a description of what you see.

And in turn, your study buddy may need you to take similar steps in order to help him learn effectively.

Pretend you're about to start working with a study buddy. To prepare for this, write in your notebook how you would go about explaining how you learn best. Begin something like this: "I learn best when I. . . . "

START WITH THE POSITIVE

Accentuate the positive and you'll feel more focused and motivated.

- In discussing each other's notes or papers, talk first about what you liked most, or what interested you. *Then* ask questions about what you found unclear or weakly supported.
- In discussing notes, a text, or a lecture, begin with what you got out of it. *Then* talk about what was confusing.

USE SENSITIVE TALK

To get the most from a relationship, especially when your purpose is to help each other, it's important you both respect each other's opinions, no matter how different they might be.

No-Fault Talking

Remember the magic word "I" from Chapter 15? When criticizing or giving an opinion, begin with "I," so that it's clear you're simply stating how you feel, not imposing a judgment. For example, instead of saying, "That answer is wrong," say something like, "I have trouble with that," or "I don't understand how you came to that conclusion."

Remember that a study partnership is a give-and-take relationship. When you use "I," you are assuming responsibility. Maybe you've heard people insist on something being right or wrong. When you're told, "You're wrong," you feel punished. When you feel punished, you don't feel like working; you might even feel like giving up. You and your partner will feel encouraged to go on if you both agree to take each other's ideas seriously. You can even agree to disagree! The difference is, you're not making anyone feel they're wrong.

Making Yourself Understood

Maybe you didn't say what you meant to say. This may very well happen at times because you think faster than you speak. How can you find out if you made yourself clear? If your buddy is shy or quiet, he might be reluctant to ask you questions or to ask you to repeat what you just said. You need to pay attention to body language to see if you're being understood. A wrinkled forehead or nose, or a blank stare are all clues. When in doubt, ask your buddy, "What did you hear me say?"

Listen Attentively

You have an important responsibility as a study buddy: Be sensitive to how your partner feels and thinks. Your partner will know you're listening when you:

- Ask questions.
- Ask to have something repeated.
- Tell her what you thought she said ("I thought you said . . . Is that what you meant?").

Imagine disagreeing with a study buddy. Using sensitive talk, write in your notebook how you might respond.

IN SHORT

To make sure that "two heads are better than one," use sensitive talk with your study buddy to explain how you feel, and to make sure you're understanding what your partner said. Tell your buddy how you learn best. Be prepared to work with your partner's learning styles, even if they're different from yours. Choose a place and time to work that's convenient for you both and free of distractions. Focus on the task at hand.

Practice Tips

The next time you're talking with someone, whether it's a family member, friend, or colleague, try using sensitive talk.

- Make sure you heard what the other person *intended* to say. After your friend or colleague has spoken, say something like, "I heard you say . . . Was that what you meant?"
- Keep in mind the magic word "I." When you disagree with something, don't state a *fact*, state your *opinion*. Personalize your reaction by saying something like, "I see it like this. . . ."
- In a notebook, write what it was like for you to use sensitive talk in everyday conversation.

Have an instant buddy session with a classmate. (Maybe you're doing this already!) After class, begin a reflective discussion. Ask somebody that you're comfortable with a question like, "What did you think of what the teacher said about the national debt in today's class?"

CHAPTER | 17

You've been working closely with your study buddy, and now you're on your own. Or, for whatever reason, you never had a study partner. What can you do to make up for the fact that you don't have anyone whom with to share ideas and interpretations, or to exchange questions and answers? You can treat yourself as your own buddy!

BEING YOUR OWN PARTNER

Many students say what they like best about working with a partner is that it takes the heat off. There's less stress when you're sharing the pressure with someone else. And two heads are often better than one. But if, for whatever reason, you don't have a study buddy, you can reap the benefits of working in a pair by pretending there's someone else in the room. You can imagine yourself as your own partner, your own coach. It's not very difficult, and it can actually be fun!

> ### What, No Study Buddy?
>
> Jill was stumped. She'd been studying sociology with Jack, and now his work schedule changed, leaving no mutual free time for them to meet. She approached other classmates, trying to begin another study-buddy relationship, but none of them had a schedule that matched hers. She was on her own.
>
> "This is a problem," she said to herself. "I need somebody to act as a sounding board to hear my thoughts and conclusions on the sociology readings. I need help coming up with an idea for my paper, and I really need somebody to get me going so that I can study for the final!"

BE YOUR OWN HELP-MATE

What did you like about working with a study buddy? (If you haven't worked with a partner yet, what do you think you'd like about working with a study buddy?)

Write your responses in your notebook or record them on your tape recorder. Then try to recreate a study buddy session using your notes.

TALK TO YOURSELF!

Since you are your own partner now, talk to yourself like your partner would; it will trigger your thinking.

- **Talk as you're planning.**
  Jill, after losing Jack as a partner, now talks to herself before tackling a new subject. She then writes in her notebook what she's expecting to read and what she knows about the subject already.

- **Talk as you're doing.**
  Jill says out loud, then writes, what makes sense to her, and what questions come to mind as she studies.

- **Talk afterwards.**

   Jill says out loud, then writes, answers to the questions she can answer, and goes back to the text for answers to the rest of her questions. She does a mini oral presentation for herself to sum up what she studied. She sometimes even records her presentation on audiotape so she can play it back and listen to herself, looking for her strengths and weaknesses.

One of the things that makes working with a buddy so helpful is that the other person is helping you make connections. The more you make connections with what you already know, the more you'll find that what you're studying sticks in your memory. A buddy might say, "That reminds me of when we were talking about. . . . " And whammy—your memory is triggered! Part of being your own buddy is giving yourself *memory triggers*. For extra help on this subject, review the tips in Chapter 11, "Remembering What You've Learned."

THE GREAT PRETENDER

Another way to be your own partner is to pretend your buddy is sitting next to you. This is especially helpful if you've been regularly working with someone else and now you're preparing for an exam on your own.

When Jill pretended Jack was studying with her, she could imagine him asking her questions and responding to her answers. She didn't feel so alone anymore, and when she was done, she felt much better prepared for the final.

Getting Ready to Study

Before you begin your next study session, clear your mind of other matters, go over what you studied in your last session, and then set the agenda for this one.

Support yourself as your buddy would. Relieve yourself of everyday worries so that you can give all your energy and attention to studying. Instead of talking to your partner, talk to yourself. Write, or talk into a tape recorder for five minutes about whatever's on your mind—how your day's going, what you need to do after the study session, or anything else that you'd want to say if you had a study buddy with you. It might seem odd at first, but it's all part of setting the scene, so to speak, of getting distractions out of the way and getting focused to study.

When this little chat session is over, review your last study session. Think about what was useful to you. Take note of what comes to mind:

- **If you learn best by seeing:** Write as you talk.

- **If you learn best by hearing:** Speak into a tape recorder.

While You're Studying

When you read a text, pretend your study buddy is there with you. What questions might he or she ask? As you answer each question, show your buddy (really yourself) where you found the answer in the text.

After You've Studied

Ask yourself what new information or better understanding came from this study session. Record your responses in your notebook or on your tape recorder. Review your notes each study session. Add answers to your questions, and then add other questions and connections as they come to mind.

GET THE MOST FROM YOUR SESSIONS

If you're going to *really* help yourself, apply the methods that worked with a partner to your sessions alone. For starters, review Chapter 16, "Working with a Study Buddy", which lists the four basic rules for a successful study session:

- Appreciate your own learning styles.
- Start with the positive.
- Use sensitive talk.
- Listen attentively.

You can apply each of these to yourself.

APPRECIATE YOUR OWN LEARNING STYLES

Since you're working alone, you only have your own learning styles to consider. This presents a good opportunity for you to make sure you're using methods of studying that are suitable for the way you learn. Be aware of what works best for you and make changes if necessary. (You may want to review Chapters 2 through 5 on learning styles.)

START WITH THE POSITIVE

Begin a session by asking yourself what you liked about what you read, wrote, saw, or heard. Starting out with something you enjoy and feel comfortable with will give you a sense of accomplishment as you say to yourself, "I know that!" Then you can face the more challenging material with a good attitude.

USE SENSITIVE TALK

Remember, you're your partner now. Keep being sensitive to your feelings! Use the magic word "I" even when talking to yourself. When you begin statements with, "I like . . ." and "I feel . . . " you're assuming responsibility for your opinions and feelings, and you're respecting yourself.

As you read the next part of this chapter, talk to yourself using sensitive talk. Pretend you're talking to your partner. Begin by saying, "What I've gotten out of this lesson so far is . . . ," adding whatever comes to mind. Continue with, "This makes me think of . . ." and keep talking until you have a good understanding of the lesson.

RESPECT YOURSELF

Be nice to yourself as you push ahead. Studying the material so that it makes sense to you is hard work! Acknowledge your challenges. One of the comforts of a buddy is that you have someone who knows what you're going through, someone who's listening to you talk about your hard day and who is also talking about his day. Play both roles yourself.

Jill tells herself something like, "I know you've had a hard day. I wish you could take the day off tomorrow; you'll look into arranging for that soon, if you can. In the meantime, is there some way you can treat yourself, maybe take a short walk or look through a magazine, before you settle down to study?"

Don't criticize yourself! Instead, *ask* yourself:

- What else do I need to know to make a clear picture in my head?

- What else do I need to know so the order of events will make sense?

IN SHORT

Whether you act like your partner or pretend your buddy is next to you, you need to acknowledge how you're feeling and the challenges before you. Then you're ready to study. Talking to yourself before, during, and after studying helps you ask questions and make connections. This in turn helps you to better understand and remember what you've studied. Keep your thoughts in a notebook or tape recorder, so that you can go over and add to them each study session.

Practice Tips

Talking to yourself while studying, and pretending you've got an invisible buddy, may seem a bit odd to you at first!

To get used to the idea and become good at it, practice before you start your study sessions.

When you're by yourself—in the shower, in the car, walking to work or school—begin a conversation with yourself. To make it seem more real, pretend you're with a classmate. Try out questions like:

- So, how was class yesterday?
- What did you find most interesting? Puzzling?
- When is your next study session?
- What do you think you'll need to spend the most time on during that session?

No one's around, so you can speak freely and pretend you're talking to anyone you want. Relax, and realize that you're doing it for a specific reason: to learn!

CHAPTER | 18

In this chapter, you'll be using what you've learned about reading closely, keeping calm, and using your learning styles to deal with tests that are generally looking for one specific answer to each question. These include true/false, matching, multiple-choice, and fill-in-the-blank tests.

PREPARING FOR SHORT-ANSWER TESTS

Many tests—classroom tests, professional tests, and school admission exams—use the multiple choice format, sometimes along with true/false, matching, or fill-in-the-blank questions. These formats are similar in that they have only one right answer.

The problem with tests that require specific answers is that you're either right or wrong; there's not much room for personal opinion. Even if you've studied and know the material thoroughly, you still may find some questions challenging. That's because these tests are often designed to be tricky: multiple-choice tests offer "close" answers in addition to the correct one; matching tests use words out of context. So in addition to knowing the subject matter, you've got to learn how to take these kinds of tests, and this includes making up your own practice test.

Getting Over Test-Taking Obstacles

Tim and Tameka had been studying for exams that would qualify them for promotions. They'd been studying for several months and were confident they knew the material. As it got closer to test time, they both began to panic because they knew they'd be given a combination of different kinds of tests.

Tim told Tameka, "I think I can handle everything but fill-in-the-blanks. I'm OK, if the right answer is there and I can find it, but I'm really stuck if I have to come up with the name of something on my own. I have trouble with names!"

Tameka said, "What about me? I get confused when I see a bunch of answers that are similar to each other and I have to choose the one that's right. I say to myself, 'Well, maybe under certain circumstances choice **A** would be correct, but then again, choice **B** would work in a different situation.' I do it every time!"

Tim has a problem coming up with the right names, and Tameka has a problem when answer choices are very similar. What Tim needs to do is learn to associate names with meanings, and Tameka needs to come up with an answer before looking at the choices.

STUDYING FOR A TEST

The best way to study for a test is to test yourself, or have your study buddy test you.

TESTING YOURSELF

Creating a test of your own forces you to think like a teacher. As you develop questions, you hone in on what's most important in what you're studying. This helps you understand the material better, and it gives you more confidence in yourself. It also helps you become more responsible for your own learning. When you make up a test like this, you are doing it for yourself; enjoy the feeling! Writing a test also helps you understand how tests are made. This can make you more comfortable when you take the real test.

TESTING WITH A PARTNER

If you're studying with a partner, make up a test for each other. Be sure to make up answer sheets on separate paper and have proof for every correct answer. If you're studying from a pamphlet or book, for example, cite the page number on which the answer can be found. When you and your partner have completed each other's test, swap. Check your partner's answers with your answer sheet and have him do the same. Go over the answers for both tests together.

CREATING QUESTIONS
Getting Ready

First, pretend you're the instructor.

Get a piece of paper, and:

1. List what you would want your students to get out of the course or book. Write as many things as you can think of.
2. Circle three items that are most important to you. These three items should represent the *general* idea of the course.
3. Circle two items that fall under each of your three main ideas. These points should be more specific; they will concern details of the course material.
4. Now you have nine items. Make each one into a question.

Questions for Your Study Buddy

If you're preparing a test for a partner you can make up any of the four types of short-answer questions. Multiple-choice questions may seem difficult to create at first. Follow this formula for choices: make up four possible answers for each question—a correct answer, a nearly correct answer, an answer loosely associated with the right answer, and an answer that is obviously wrong.

Questions for Yourself

Fill-in-the-blank questions can be used to help you learn definitions of new vocabulary you encounter while studying. You can also prepare multiple-choice, true/false, and matching questions to simulate the actual test you'll be taking. Although you'll probably be able to answer such questions easily since you made them up, the process of creating the questions will give you new insights into correct answers—and help you predict what tricks you'll see on the real test.

Get a piece of paper and write the answers to the following questions. If you tested yourself:

- What did you do to make up the test?
- Which was more comfortable for you, making the questions or making the answers?
- Which answers were easiest to come up with?

If you worked with a partner:

- Which was more comfortable for you, creating the test or answering your partner's test?
- What did you do to complete the test?
- Which questions were easiest for you to answer?

PROCESS OF ASSOCIATION

As you study, try using large index cards for terms and ideas you could be tested on. Write big so key words will stick in your mind. Use a different color for each category. For instance, in a Spanish class, you might use one color for the names of foods, another color for the names of kinds of businesses, and a different color for the names of articles of furniture.

Next, come up with associations between these unfamiliar words and ideas and things that are more familiar to you. Ask yourself, "What does this word remind me of?" It all depends on you; whatever comes to *your* mind works. The more unusual the association is, the more likely it is to stick with you. Maybe it's an image of something you see every day, like a tree or a pancake. Or maybe it's something a little stranger: perhaps the word *cognitive* makes you think of a giant purple cog on top of a person's head. Maybe it's the name of a celebrity or politician. Maybe it's a configuration of numbers. Whatever your association is, write it on your card with the term or idea you need to learn. Carry the cards with you to review at opportune times—for instance, on the bus, on the exercise bike, and while waiting in line.

- **If you learn best by using images:** Draw any images that you associate with the information on each card. Use your imagination!

- **If you learn best by seeing:** Tape up your index cards in places you can't miss, for example, on the bedroom and bathroom mirrors and by the front door. Use colors to highlight key words.

- **If you learn best by hearing:** Sing the words on your cards, even if you're not an opera star. This will make the association more unique, and it will get another part of your brain operating. What you *sing* stays with you longer than what you *say*.

There are probably other wacky but effective things you can do; use your imagination. Only *you* think like you!

PREPARE YOURSELF FOR THE TEST
KEEPING CALM

Even before the test day there are things you can do to quell test anxiety. You may want to review Chapter 1, "Getting Started," for tips on keeping calm. You feel calmer when you're satisfied that you've studied as much as possible. You may also want to review Chapter 7, "Knowing What You Know," for tips on making sure you're as prepared as you think you are. Eating nourishing meals will help; so does getting a good night's sleep.

Shortly before taking the test:

- Imagine yourself in a soothing place. Close your eyes, and enjoy the smells, sounds, and feelings of this out-of-the-way spot. It can be a place you actually have been to, a place you've seen in a photograph or movie, or somewhere that your imagination has created.

- Breathe slowly and deeply as you are imagining this place. Open your eyes when you feel calm.

If you can practice this exercise several times during the days before the test, it will be easier to visualize the place if anxiety sets in.

PSYCHING YOURSELF

Now that you're calm, cool, and collected, you're ready to concentrate. Remind yourself that you've studied carefully. Some people like to use their imagination to help them concentrate and to help remind them that they know the material they've studied. You could pretend you're the instructor (or even the textbook!) and visualize that all the material is inside you. When you can picture something like this in your head, you're better able to hold your concentration.

A TESTY SITUATION

Each of the following test formats has its own way of being tricky. The best way to learn how they work is to practice. The more tests you take, the easier it will be for you to weed out wrong answers.

MULTIPLE CHOICE

A multiple-choice test can be tricky. Often, you have four possible answer choices. Usually, they follow this pattern:

- One answer is correct.
- One answer is close to the correct answer.
- One answer is very different from the correct answer.
- One answer is loosely associated with the correct answer but is not close.

TRUE/FALSE

A true/false test works on a similar principle. The contrast between your two choices can be great or small; your options can be direct opposites or one can be close but not quite correct.

MATCHING

A matching test is similar to multiple-choice in that the answer is there, but you have to find it among answers that may be close in definition. Some matching tests have more choices in one column than in the other. It's important you read the directions very carefully so you don't get confused by extra choices.

FILL-IN-THE-BLANK

A fill-in-the-blank test is the opposite of a matching or multiple-choice test. The answer is not there for you; you have to come up with it yourself. The best way to prepare for this type of test is to know your vocabulary—including correct spelling.

READING CLOSELY TO FIND THE CORRECT ANSWER

Your first clue to a right answer is in reading the question closely. (You might want to review Chapter 10, "Getting More out of Reading.") You need to find out *exactly* what a question is asking. As you read the test question:

- What questions come to mind?
- What images or words come to mind?

USE YOUR LEARNING STYLE

As always, use the style that suits you best to approach a question. (You may want to review Chapters 2 through 5 on learning styles.)

- **If you learn best by hearing:** Read the question out loud (softly, if others are nearby!).

- **If you learn best by seeing:** Use scrap paper to write down key words or draw a picture that comes to mind.

- **If you learn best by using images:** Turn the question into a picture or movie in your head. Ask yourself: "What's needed to complete the picture?"

1.
2.
3.

- **If you learn best by putting things in order:** Imagine the question as a puzzle or comic strip. Ask yourself: "Which of the choices would make the most sense and complete the puzzle?"

- **If you learn best by doing:** Imagine yourself acting out the question. Hold on to the picture of you in your head. Ask yourself: "Which of the two choices would you pick in that situation?"

HOW TO APPROACH THE QUESTIONS

Start by quickly skimming through the test to find the questions that are easiest for you. You'll save time if you do challenging questions later. Remember, only correct answers count! If your test is timed, you'll get more correct answers down on paper by doing the ones you know for sure first.

Tackle each question, one at a time.

1. When you read the question, cover up your choice of answers. Think only of the question. What answer comes to mind? Hold on to the answer in your head, or write it down if you're permitted to use scrap paper.
2. Now look for the answer among the choices given that comes *closest* to your answer. When you know the answer, not looking at the choices first can save you time. Answer all the easy questions this way.

After you've answered all the questions you know for sure, go back to the challenging ones. Begin by picking a question you feel more comfortable with and read it again. Sometimes a bell will go off in your head the second time around. If you're working with a matching section, you've probably already eliminated some possible choices by answering the easy questions. On a multiple-choice test, if you're still not sure of the answer:

1. Rule out the answer that's not close at all.
2. Rule out the answer that's loosely associated, but not close.

3. Now you have to choose between one answer that's correct and one answer that's very close. You're making an *educated guess* here. Use your learning style! (See the suggestions above.)

Choose one answer to the practice question below:

A worker who is cognizant of her learning strengths, no matter what job she is doing, is more apt to do well.

In the sentence above, *cognizant* most nearly means

    a.   proud
    b.   aware
    c.   highly knowledgeable
    d.   automated

Making an Educated Guess

Use your learning style to make sense of the question.

- **If you learn best by using images:** See a picture of a worker doing her job well.

- **If you learn best by putting things in order:** Imagine the different steps involved in getting a job done well.

- **If you learn best by doing:** Imagine yourself doing very competent work.

In the question above, maybe you ruled out the "way out" answer, **d,** right away. Answer **a** might be a result of doing good work, but it doesn't define cognizant. Looking quickly, you might have thought, "*Cognizant*—well, it has something to do with knowing, so the answer is **c.**" But **c** is the trick answer—the answer that is *almost* correct. A trick answer can confuse you if you don't read carefully. The word *cognizant* is connected with knowledge, but it simply means being aware, not highly knowledgeable. To do a job well, you have to be aware of how you work best. The correct answer then, is **b.**

In Short

To do the best you can on an test, keep calm, read carefully, and answer shrewdly. Begin by answering questions you know for sure. Then go back to the tougher ones, starting with those that are the least difficult. When you know fill-in-the-blanks will be included, practice beforehand by making your own associations with the words and terms you might be tested on. Carry the cards with you and tape them up where you'll see them. Explore the techniques that work best with your learning style.

Practice Tip

As you read—a magazine in the barber shop, a newspaper on your way to work, a message on the TV screen—choose a word that seems important in a particular sentence. Create an association with that word, something that will help the word stick with you. Practicing in everyday situations will make coming up with associations easier; then you'll be able to study more efficiently.

CHAPTER | 19

Taking an essay test involves several steps: reviewing the whole test first, deciding how much time to spend on each question, carefully reading each question and answering it fully, and finally, checking each answer.

PREPARING FOR ESSAY TESTS

An essay test asks questions that can't be answered in short, simple facts. Each question requires that you think about the answer and spend time answering it in writing, but there is a lot you can do in advance. The Boy Scouts have a motto: Be prepared! Before the test, you can prepare for both direct and indirect questions by asking yourself (or, if you have a study buddy, asking each other) questions directly from the text and questions based on the text and writing down your answers. Begin by reviewing Chapter 15, "Making Yourself Understood."

Use Your Study Styles

Mathilda is studying to be an accountant and she just learned she'll have to take an essay test to complete the class. Her math teacher wants to see how she thinks and solves problems. "But I just work with numbers!" she says. "I don't need to write in this job!" What Mathilda will see is that she can use her strength as someone who works best with order as a sequential *learner* to become a sequential *writer*.

GETTING READY

A good way to prepare yourself for an essay question is to write a mock test ahead of time. By acting (creating questions) and not just reacting (answering questions), you become involved in the test preparation process. To begin, pretend you're the instructor:

- Make a list of what you want your students to get out of the course and the class materials, such as hand-outs, pamphlets, and books.
- Circle the three items you feel are most important to the course.
- Make up a question for each of these items. If you're working with a study buddy, each make up your own list and separate questions. Include both direct questions, which are answered by facts from your notes or text, and at least one indirect question, which is based on how you put facts together to come up with a conclusion.
- Write an answer to each question. If you're working with a study buddy, swap the tests you made and take each other's test. Make sure you each have an answer sheet that includes page numbers that indicate where the answers can be found in your class material.

TIME MANAGEMENT

You want to make the most of the time allotted for taking the test so that you have sufficient time for answering and checking each question before the time is up.

IF THE WHOLE TEST IS ESSAY QUESTIONS

For an all-essay-question test:

- Read the entire test over before you start to answer any questions.
- Count the number of questions and make note of how much time you have left to complete the test. Give yourself a rough time limit for each question; this includes time for checking and correcting your answers!
- First answer the easiest questions.
- When you go back to answer tougher questions, begin with ones you're more comfortable with. There's bound to be some that seem less difficult than others. Sometimes writing on a topic you know well reminds you of something you'd forgotten. A "bell" might go off in your head, making a tough question easier to answer.

IF ONLY PART OF THE TEST IS ESSAY QUESTIONS

Be on the lookout for certain parts of the test that count more heavily than others. For example, maybe an essay counts for 50 percent of the test grade, a multiple-choice section 25 percent, and a fill-in-the-blank section 25 percent. While you want to spend your time where the largest percentage is, it still makes sense to go to those questions whose answers come to you first. It's OK to do most tests out of order.

KEEP CALM

Sometimes even a topic you know well seems strange and confusing when you're nervous. Take deep breaths, relax. (You may want to review the tips for keeping calm in Chapter 1, "Getting Started.") If the test is going to be several hours long, see if you're permitted to bring some juice or a bottle of water with you. And if there's a chance you might be cold, bring along a sweater. You don't have to wear it, but you'll be happy you have it if you feel chilly. Being comfortable can help you stay calm.

UNDERSTANDING THE TEST QUESTION

The first step in successfully answering an essay question is making sure you understand what it's asking! This may seem obvious but it's not unusual for test-takers under pressure to misread questions. You may want to review Chapter 10, "Getting More Out of Reading." Also, see the section below on reading different kinds of essay questions.

TYPES OF QUESTIONS

Some questions ask you something directly, such as "Where and when did such-and-such happen?" Others are more indirect, like "If such-and-such had not happened, what might the situation be today?" A question might—or might not—have been discussed in class or in the text you read.

Direct Questions

If the question is direct, you know what you're being asked and how to go about answering it. There's usually only one correct answer.

Indirect Questions

If it's an indirect question, you have to figure out what is being asked. Usually there is not one correct answer but several possible answers, depending upon your interpretation, opinion, or reaction to the question and the subject matter. What often helps in figuring out your answer to an indirect question is to try to get the *feeling* of the question. In the example, "If such-and-such had not happened, what might the situation be today?" ask yourself what kind of a feeling you would you have if such-and-such had not happened? Write down the feeling, then explain why you had that feeling.

COMING UP WITH THE ANSWER
GETTING THE IDEA

An advantage of an essay test is that extended writing actually gets you to think more clearly than just writing a one- or two-word answer. When you write, you're using much of your brain. You may want to use scrap paper to write quickly everything you know about the question as soon as you read it. Or you may want to write an outline, "talk" to yourself about the question (but not aloud; your fellow test-takers won't appreciate it!), or perhaps visualize the answer first.

If it's an indirect question, keep in mind that your opinion counts. Close your eyes for a few seconds to clear your head and let the answer come to you. On scrap paper, jot down the important facts that will prove your answer. Draw lines or number the facts to help you make connections and determine which facts you want to use in your answer and in what order they should be presented.

USE YOUR LEARNING STYLE TO CLARIFY YOUR ANSWER

The way you plan what you're going to say depends on what works best for you. For any learning style, you want to have a clear idea of the whole answer—your complete response to the question—*before* you actually write it, whether it's a few sentences or a few pages long.

Since she learns best through order, as a sequential thinker, Mathilda, (see box) found that if she made a numbered outline, she could see the order of what she'd be writing, and it would make a lot more sense to her. Then, she would write sentences describing each category in her outline. If she had been a global thinker who worked best with images, she would have written or drawn questions and ideas, and then linked them with lines or numbers. In other words, the sequential thinker thinks in order first, the global thinker thinks in order last.

- **If you learn best by hearing:** Try saying a sentence out loud (softly!) before writing it down.

- **If you learn best by seeing:** Try drawing or writing down ideas on scrap paper before you write the essay.

- **If you learn best by doing:** Imagine yourself acting out your answers. It's OK to make small movements with your hands in most testing situations, so take advantage of this opportunity. Then start writing what you're acting out.

- **If you learn best by order:** Let your writing describe the order of events you are remembering.

- **If you learn best by images:** Let your writing describe the picture that's in your head.

Get a piece of paper, and for three minutes write whatever comes to mind when you think of the word *test*. If you're stuck at first, write, "I'm stuck." Keep writing! As you write, you're remembering what you saw, and maybe felt, in different testing situations. This little exercise demonstrates how the process of writing gets you to do some brainstorming on your own, helping you think of more things as you continue to write.

Does your writing come out as a list? Or did you draw pictures? Does your method of writing tell you anything about your learning style?

WHAT MAKES WRITING MAKE SENSE?

Reading is the flip side of writing. What makes something work for you as a reader is the same thing that helps your writing make sense.

Think about something you really enjoyed reading. Anything at all—a newspaper or magazine article, a short story, a book. Maybe you just finished reading it. Maybe you read it last year. Write in your notebook what it was and why you liked it.

Now think about what you expect as a reader from anything you read. Write in your notebook whatever comes to mind.

Maybe your list looks like this:

- Has to hold my interest
- Must make sense
- Must get my imagination going
- Order of events has to make sense
- Has to use language I understand
- Has to use correct spelling and punctuation

Refer to this list every time you are about to begin a paper. Make sure your writing meets the expectations you have for other authors. Planning your essay before you write will actually save you time in the correcting phase.

WHEN IS THE QUESTION ANSWERED?

If your answer doesn't raise any further questions, and if it brings a clear picture to mind, you've probably given a sufficient answer. You can check to see if your answer is complete by making up a question from your answer. How close is your question to the real question? You may want to review Chapter 7, "Knowing What You Know"; and Chapter 8, "Knowing When You Don't Know."

CORRECTING YOUR WRITING

All writers find that they think a lot faster than they write. This means there are often words missing, or extra words, or word endings on the paper that the writer did not plan to put there. As you know, nobody can write as fast as they think! So once you've written down your answer to an essay question, you should go back over it to correct it. It's usually OK (and expected!) to mark up the exam book, showing where you want a sentence or paragraph to go, crossing out words you don't want, and the like.

Use Your Learning Style to Polish Your Writing

In the revising and editing phase of your essay test, you can still use your strongest learning style.

- **If you learn best by hearing:** Read what you've written softly to yourself. Read slowly and carefully. Listen to your own voice. Pretend you're the exam grader. Is what you're hearing the meaning you meant to convey?

- **If you learn best by seeing:** Carefully and slowly read what you've written, looking carefully for spelling, grammar, and content errors.

- **If you learn best by order:** Grammar probably comes to you more easily than spelling. Check your spelling by reading softly to yourself; take it word by word so you don't miss any subtle mistakes.

- **If you learn best by using images:** You're on order alert. First check that the descriptions you've written follow a clear order, before you check grammar and spelling. As you read softly to yourself, compare what you see with what you hear.

- **If you learn best by doing or moving:** Check your grammar by softly tapping your foot to the rhythm of what you wrote, feeling for when the beat doesn't match what's familiar. This is another way of associating what you see with what you hear. Check your spelling by following along in writing with a pencil eraser and reading softly to yourself. Also look out for missing words—you might have been writing fast, in an attempt to keep up with your thinking!

Remember—your own learning style is a combination! You might also have discovered other ways of writing and correcting that work for you.

For example, let's make up a sentence someone could have written on an imaginary test question about steam-engine regulations. Maybe you were thinking, and thought you wrote, "Those rules don't apply anymore." But, since the writing was trying to keep up with the thinking, what you wrote was something like, "Those rules aply anymore." By reading out loud carefully and slowly, you could hear the missing *don't* and see the missing *p* in *apply*. Whenever you say to yourself, "That doesn't sound right," or "That doesn't look right," go back and check. Check for anything on the paper that is different from what you are saying. You want to make sure what you're reading is the same as what you were thinking!

IN SHORT

On an essay test, you're answering specific questions. First, you need to understand what's being asked of you. Then, you need to come up with specific answers. You focus on the meaning, on the idea, of what you want to say so the reader knows what you think and feel. After you're satisfied with what your writing is saying, you then check that what you've written looks and sounds the way you want it to. Since it's a test, you'll first answer the questions you know for sure, and save the more challenging ones for later. This will save you time and energy!

Practice Tips

Practice writing "on call," without having much time to prepare. Write several questions you could imagine being asked on an essay exam. Cut each one into a strip, putting all the strips in a jar. Make a note of the time. Pull a strip out of the jar and answer the question written on it, using some of the suggestions in this chapter. Remember to:

- Use your learning style to help you come up with an answer.
- Answer it fully.
- Check that the images and order make sense.
- Check your grammar and spelling.

Note the time again. How long did it take you to finish your answer? Are you likely to have more or less time on the real test? On another day, repeat this exercise, choosing a new question and also timing your answer.

Now's the time to retake the TEST YOUR STUDY SMARTS SURVEY, if you've read all of this book through this page. If you've been reading according to what interests you, or what you feel you need, WAIT until you have completed the entire book before retaking the survey.

If you answered the questions on the first survey carefully and honestly, you'll get a clearer picture of what you know about how you learn—and what you now do about it—by waiting until you have finished the book. It's comparing your answers to the same questions, before and after reading the book, that shows you the progress you've made! (What's tricky is that if you answered the questions quickly, without much thought the first time, and now, the second time, you answer them carefully, you may not have an accurate register.)

TEST YOUR STUDY SMARTS SURVEY

<u>Circle the number that reflects how you feel, or the likeliness of what you do or don't do.</u> There are no "right" or "wrong" answers. (Remember, it's important to think carefully and to respond accurately for the survey to work!)

As the numbers go up, it means the feeling, or likeliness, increases. Number 1 means "dread"—you feel awful. Number 2 means you're not dreading it, but you feel pretty uncomfortable. Number 3 means you feel a little uncomfortable. Number 4 is neutral—you don't care one way or the other. Number 5 means you feel a little comfortable, but not very much. Number 6 means you feel pretty comfortable. Number 7 means "delight"—you feel terrific, couldn't feel better.

For each question, think about being in a learning or studying situation, such as being in a class.

<u>If you spoke another language before English, do this section first.</u> If English is your *first* language, skip this section. Think about your feelings towards your first language, your "mother tongue."

How do you feel about reading?	1	2	3	4	5	6	7
How do you feel about listening?	1	2	3	4	5	6	7
How do you feel about writing?	1	2	3	4	5	6	7
How do you feel about speaking?	1	2	3	4	5	6	7

<u>In this section, think about how you feel using English.</u>

How do you feel about reading?	1	2	3	4	5	6	7
How do you feel about listening?	1	2	3	4	5	6	7
How do you feel about writing?	1	2	3	4	5	6	7
How do you feel about speaking?	1	2	3	4	5	6	7
How do you feel about math?	1	2	3	4	5	6	7
How do you feel about algebra?	1	2	3	4	5	6	7

For this section, circle the answer that you feel applies to you now.

Are you comfortable working with others?

  Never   Rarely   Sometimes   Usually

Do you take notes (in writing or on cassette tape) while you read or listen?

  Never   Rarely   Sometimes   Usually

Do you ask yourself questions as you read or listen?

  Never   Rarely   Sometimes   Usually

Do you ask yourself questions as you write or calculate?

  Never   Rarely   Sometimes   Usually

Do you make pictures in your head as you read or listen?

  Never   Rarely   Sometimes   Usually

Do you make pictures in your head as you write or calculate?

  Never   Rarely   Sometimes   Usually

Do you re-read what you've written?

  Never   Rarely   Sometimes   Usually

Do you read what you've written out loud?

  Never   Rarely   Sometimes   Usually

Now's the time to FIND OUT THE DIFFERENCE between how you studied before reading this book and how you're studying (and feeling about studying) now.

Go back to page xiii, at the end of the Introduction, and compare your answers. What do you think?

CHAPTER | 20

As you've seen throughout this book, everyone learns differently. Everyone has strong and weak areas of the brain. But what if your weak area is really weak, so weak that it's preventing you from accomplishing your goals, even when you're working hard? This chapter helps you figure out when you need help with a learning difference that may be a learning disability.

KNOWING WHEN YOU NEED HELP

Everyone learns in unique ways. Remember how Chapter 2, "Discovering How You Learn," described us all as learning seesaws? It's unusual for anyone's seesaw to be perfectly level. It's up on the side where you're a strong learner, and down where your learning is less strong.

If your seesaw is very tilted because you've got a super-strong learning style that's bringing that side all the way up, you're often paying a price for it. In order to balance out that super strength, another learning style may be difficult for you. Everyone has a learning difference. But in some people, the difference is so pronounced it gets in the way of learning. An extreme weakness in acquiring or expressing knowledge is called a learning disability. If you have a learning disability, you're not alone; 8 to 15 percent of people in the U.S. have some kind of learning disability.

COMPENSATING FOR A DISABILITY

In Chapters 2 through 5, you looked at the different ways people learn. In Chapters 7 and 8, you thought about when you know something for sure, and when something's not clear to you. You may want to review these chapters before continuing. For example, someone who is a real whiz in math, and very strong on order—a sequential learner—might have little interest in reading stories or watching fictional movies. Or, someone could be an amazing auditory learner, learning predominately by hearing, yet have difficulty spelling. For most people, strengths and weaknesses balance each other out.

Most people who have a learning disability don't know that they have it. They know, on some level, that something's not quite right, but they've naturally been compensating for it. The person who is uncomfortable reading, for example, might be an avid radio listener and an engaging speaker.

Those who do know they have a learning disability are often unclear about what it is. Perhaps they were diagnosed in grammar or high school, perhaps they were even in special classes or met regularly with an educational specialist, but they still might not know exactly why they were there. And, often those who know what kind of learning disability they have don't know what to do about it.

The solution is to find out how you learn best, to know when you need help, and to know where to go to get it!

GETTING HELP

You've already begun helping yourself, even before you started reading this book. You are making up for your learning difficulty in some way, even if you don't know it. Your brain does this to protect and help you. But there's a limit to how much compensating your mind can do. You may have a learning difficulty if you often find yourself saying things like this:

- I know the words in this sentence, but I just can't make sense of it.
- I know this person is talking, but I don't understand what they're talking about.
- I recognize the numbers and math signs, but I don't know how to do the problem.
- I know I knew it once, but I don't know what it is now.

OUTSIDE HELP

There are organizations listed in the Appendix that you may find useful. But help might be closer than you think.

Some schools and companies have tutoring available. They may also have consultants you can talk with. Often, these people can put you in touch with a learning specialist.

- If you're with a company, check your human resources department.
- If you're with a school, check the advisement and counseling offices.

When your seesaw is tilted to the point that your weaker way of learning is damaging your self-confidence and keeping you from accomplishing your goals, you may have a learning disability. Most people with learning disabilities have average or above-average intelligence. If this is you, you're in good company. Albert Einstein, who made a great impact on physics, but couldn't count his change for the bus; and Winston Churchill, who made a great political and historical impact, but couldn't spell, are just two of the world's geniuses who had learning disabilities.

WHAT DO I LOOK FOR?

TYPES OF DISABILITIES

While there are many, many different kinds of learning disabilities, you'll read only about the common ones here. See the Appendix for sources of more information on all types.

If you should be diagnosed as having a learning disability (or combination of disabilities), you might feel relieved. "Ah!" you might say, "there's a name for this and it can be dealt with!"

Dyslexia

Harold is dyslexic. His eyes see just fine, but the message from his eyes to his brain sometimes gets interrupted. Letters sometimes look like they're dancing on the page. Harold has to pay close attention to what he reads, and when he can, he gets books and hand-outs printed in large type. A tutor helped him learn to break words down into parts so he could read out loud and spell with fewer errors. He pays such close attention that he can read a page upside-down.

Auditory Processing Difficulties

Tami's ears hear fine, but the message from her ears to her brain is sometimes garbled and sounds like she's listening on a phone with a poor connection. Sometimes it comes through clearly, sometimes not. She deals with this by taking notes and asking questions. She also asks teachers to write on the board and give her hand-outs.

Attention Deficit Disorder

Maude was born with an excessive need for attention, and she usually has difficulty paying attention to something for longer than ten minutes at a time. But for those ten minutes, she can really concentrate. She asks permission to sit by the instructor, so she'll be less likely to be distracted. She has learned to live with distraction; in fact, she has learned to use it to her advantage. She can work on several projects at the same time.

Short-Term Memory Difficulties

It is a real challenge for Jake to remember something recently said. He deals with it by carrying a notepad with him at all times, writing down what he wants to remember. When he's listening to a lecture, he tapes it so he can later replay it, a few minutes at a time. Each time he listens, he writes down what he wants to remember.

GET TO KNOW YOUR STRENGTHS AND WEAKNESSES

Generally, we can all use help when it comes to learning. It's rare that any of us have perfectly balanced seesaws. Be aware of when you're understanding a concept you're working to figure out. Keep a log of what's happening to you. Look for patterns—of situations that are troublesome and situations that are helpful. Write in your log at least once each day. After a week or two, you should have a clearer picture of how you learn.

If you are meeting with someone at your school or workplace such as a learning consultant, psychologist, or tutor, bring your log and review it with her. The service is usually free for you. When you take an active part in diagnosing your learning weakness, you'll be better able to control it, and even use it to your advantage.

IN SHORT

You're a unique learner. You're different from everyone else—and everyone else is different from everyone else! Each of us has a learning difference. When you realize how your seesaw of learning strength and weakness operates, you can use your strength to get a handle on the learning weakness. You might even find a way to use it to your advantage!

Practice Tip

Keep track of yourself daily! When are you at your best: most confident, focused, and clear-headed? What is it that distracts you when you try to concentrate?

In a notebook, track yourself for at least a week. If it's reading you're concerned about, focus on reading. Concentrate on making things a little more comfortable than usual. For example, if you're eating cereal and reading the box and you suddenly realize that reading is easier for you than usual, write down the situation: "yellow box, green large letters, my eyes looking down." You may very well find that switching to large-type books is a help, and so is using yellow note paper instead of white. If you discover that you're really enjoying your new class because the teacher often explains concepts in big circles with connecting lines between them, make note of it and try to repeat it in other learning situations.

APPENDIX

ADDITIONAL RESOURCES

As you've discovered, there are many parts to studying! Learning how you learn, knowing when you understand something and when you don't, making questions, finding answers, dealing with different classroom situations, preparing for different kinds of tests, speaking and writing so others will understand what you mean—these are all parts of the study process. Check the following lists for publications and organizations useful to you in all these steps.

In addition to the nationally available resources listed here, your area is likely to have similar resources. For instance, many public libraries run programs that offer reading help. Check with your local library, high school, or community college to find out what's available in your area.

BASIC SKILLS: WRITING AND READING

Educational Solutions, Inc.
99 University Place
New York, NY 10003
212-674-2988

Assorted materials on math, ESL, reading, speaking, spelling, and related topics are available.

Becoming A Writer **by Bill Bernhardt and Peter Miller (St. Martin's Press, 1986)**

Now out of print, but excerpts are available from the authors at
The College of Staten Island
2800 Victory Boulevard
Staten Island, NY 10314
Uses writing exercises to get you to want to write, to be aware of writing, and to edit your work.

Writing With Power, 2nd Ed., **by Peter Elbow (Oxford University Press, 1998)**

Helps you get your words on paper and teaches you to write clearly and effectively.

The Least You Should Know About English, **6th ed., by Teresa F. Glazier (Holt, Rinehart and Winston, 1997)**

Helps you straighten out words that look or sound like other words.

The Elements of Style **by William Strunk, Jr., and E. B. White (Allyn and Bacon, 1995)**

Helps you keep track of standard American syntax and grammar.

Read Better, Remember More, **2 ed. by Elizabeth Chesla (LearningExpress, 2000)**

(order information at the back of this book)
Shows you how to remember what you read by helping you better understand what you read.

Grammar Essentials, 2 ed. by Judith F. Olson (LearningExpress, 2000)
(order information at the back of this book)
Gives you all the essentials of standard grammar in an easy-to-use format.

STUDY SKILLS AND TEST-TAKING

Ace Any Test, 3rd ed., by Ronald W. Fry (Career Press, 1996)
A quick and irreverent guide to test-taking, aimed at high school and college students but also good for adults.

How to Learn Anything Quickly: An Accelerated Program for Rapid Learning by Ricki Linksman (Citadel Press, 1996)
Like the book you have in your hand, this one focuses on learning styles, going into right- and left-brained thinking in more detail.

The Secrets of Taking Any Test, 2 ed. by Judith Meyers (LearningExpress, 2000)
(order information at the back of this book)
Specifically for adult learners, this book shows you how to get organized and gives you tips on taking all kinds of tests, from classroom tests to civil service or licensure and certificate exams.

LEARNING DISABILITIES
The following organizations can put you in touch with people or organizations in your area for evaluations, support groups, training programs, advocacy and legal rights, and more. Call or write for free information.

Learning Disabilities Association of America
4156 Library Road
Pittsburgh, PA 15234
412-341-1515

National Center for Learning Disabilities
381 Park Avenue South, Suite 1401
New York, NY 10016
888-575-7373 phone; 212-545-9665 fax
website: *www.ncld.org*

The Orton Dyslexia Society
71 West 23rd Street, Suite 1500
New York, NY 10010
800-222-3123 or 212-691-1930

Parents' Educational Resource Center
Charles and Helen Schwab Foundation
1660 South Amphlett, Suite 200
San Mateo, CA 94402
800-471-9545 or 415-655-2410
website: *www.perc-schwabfdn.org*

Children and Adults with Attention Deficit Disorder (CH.A.D.D.)
499 N.W. 70th Avenue, Suite 101
Plantation, FL 33317-9952
website: *http://www.chadd.org*

You might want to try this helpful book:
***Driven to Distraction* by Edward Hallowell and John Ratey (Pantheon Books, 1995)**
    True stories of people in different jobs and situations who have attention deficit disorder.